BOB IZUMI'S
BIG
BASS
BOOK

A COMPLETE GUIDE TO BASS FISHING

BOB IZUMI WITH TOM PAWLICK

KEY PORTER·BOOKS

*To my father Joe Izumi and my wife Sandy for encouraging
me to fish for a living.*

B.I.

For Tuyet, who catches more fish than I do.

T.P.

Canadian Cataloguing in Publication Data

Izumi, Bob
   Bob Izumi's big bass book

Includes index.
ISBN 1-55013-016-1

1. Bass fishing.   I. Pawlick, Thomas.   II. Title.
III. Title: Big bass book.

SH681.I98 1987   799.1'758   C87093125-3

Key Porter Books Limited
70 The Esplanade
Toronto, Ontario
Canada M5E 1R2

Illustrations: Curtis Atwater
Design: Elaine Macpherson Enterprises Limited
Typesetting: Trigraph Inc.
Printed and bound in Canada by T.H. Best
Photo Credits: All photographs are by Sandy Izumi and
Wayne Izumi with the exception of the following: pages
29, 30, 33, 35, 37 (Shimano) and pages 40 and 86
(Dupont).

87 88 89 90 6 5 4 3 2 1

CONTENTS

PREFACE

For me, bass fishing begins with Rondeau
Bay—a real place, a memory and an inspiration all
rolled up in one. Actually, it's not so much a bay as
a sort of bend in the north shore of Lake Erie, east
of Leamington, Ontario, but when I was a kid it had
some of the best fishing in Canada. I caught my first
bass there, entered my first derby and first tournament, and witnessed in microcosm the whole evolu-
tion of modern sport fishing.

Thanks to my family, especially my Dad, Joe
Izumi, I found my life's work there. You could say
it's not only where I came from, but where I'm still
coming from—and where pro bass fishing in Canada
really came from as well.

I remember wading out in the water off Rondeau pier, barefoot in the sand, when I was only four
years old, fishing for bluegills with my brother
Wayne. We'd put two hooks on our line at once and
bait them with dry flies (Wayne had a fly rod), bits
of worm or minnows. Every now and then a bass
would come cruising past, spot one of our minnows,
move right up and suck it in as we watched. A fish
is a fish to a little kid, but even then it was something
special when that happened.

When we got a little older, we'd fish off the
banks for largemouth with the bait-casting rods we
won in the Rondeau Rod and Gun Club fishing
derbies, going out at night and throwing Jitterbugs
in the dark. At first the rods were tubular steel or

hexagonal steel—the state of the art in those days—with wooden handles. Then fiberglass came in, at first solid then hollow-tube fiberglass, and we won ourselves a bunch of those. We never bought tackle. We used what we won in those early kids' derbies. Over the years, the prizes kept getting better, the tackle became more advanced, the bass bigger—and we never stopped learning.

When I was 12 we got our first boat, a bright orange homemade plywood punt lined with fiberglass. A friend, George McTavish, and I bought it from a neighbor for $25—$12.50 apiece. It was a major investment. We felt obliged to find as many uses for it as we could, to make it pay off, and painted it camo-brown for duck hunting. I don't recall that we actually used it for hunting, but we caught a heck of a lot of bass from that little eight-footer. We'd put in at Shrewsbury, row out in the bay and catch lunkers like you wouldn't believe. That boat was so small, like a cork on the water, that a couple of times when we nailed a four-pounder it would actually tow the boat. It was there that we tried out the first plastic worms when they were introduced, purple worms rigged Texas-style, and watched them murder the largemouths. My Dad went crazy with them, swore by them. He thought they were the only bass bait in the world, better than a real nightcrawler in the weeds.

We were storing up memories and storing up knowledge at the same time, learning from experience and from our friends and neighbors who, like us, lived and breathed fishing. The Reverend Thomas was typical.

Shrewsbury had once been a stopping point on the Underground Railroad that smuggled slaves out of the United States in the 1860s, and a lot of blacks lived in the town. The Reverend Thomas (he wasn't a minister and I never did find out why they called him that) was black and ran a little store there, a sort of shack where he sold ice cream, candy and bait, rented boats and made the biggest hamburgers in the world. Cooked with a big Spanish onion on top, they were juicy and super-good. I'll never forget the time I went in to get one and he was complaining that the food inspectors had been bothering him. "Oh, I've just been hit by those so-and-so's and I have to move the nightcrawlers out of the kitchen!" he said. He was hopping mad. He had to build a little wall to separate his live bait counter from the lunch counter, and he was sure it would be the downfall of his business.

The first pro bass tournament in Canada was held in Rondeau Bay and was organized by my father. Of course I entered it. I didn't take first place, but by then I was already hooked on bass as bad as any fish was ever hooked on my lure. I think the deciding point came somewhere around my thirteenth year, walking in waders along the roads in Shrewsbury in the spring when high water had come up over the banks and the bass had come with it. You could see them in the crystal-clear water, swimming right along the roads, and I made up my mind they were the fish for me.

The decision to turn pro came much later, and my life on the tournament circuit didn't begin in earnest until I was a grown man. But Rondeau Bay started it—the water, the fish and my Dad. I'm grateful to them all, and if this book goes part of the way toward giving somebody else the same kind of memories and love of the sport that bend in the Lake Erie shore gave me, I'll have gone a little way toward paying them back in kind.

B.I.

ONE

BIG JAWS AND LITTLE JAWS

The honorable name of bass has been bestowed on many species of fish in North America—from the scrappy little rock bass, pulled in by the thousands every summer by legions of kids fishing with hooks and worms, to the famed striper bass, sought by surf casters along the Atlantic and Pacific coasts. But of all the fish that carry the bass label, without a doubt the best-known and most respected by Canadian and American anglers alike are the largemouth (known to scientists as *Micropterus salmoides*) and the smallmouth (*Micropterus dolomieui*).

Big Jaws and Little Jaws—these two game fighters are by far my own favorite fish, as well as the preferred quarry of some of the best anglers ever to wet a line. Pursuing them has been the pastime of such all-time great sportsmen and keen tournament competitors as Bill Dance, Al Lindner, Jimmy Houston and my own brother Wayne, who rates the bass clan a fitting challenge for even the sharpest-witted fisherman.

The sheer number of different situations, puzzles and problems, changes of habitat and switches of mood offered by bass is unmatched by any other species. In a single lake in June, for example, there may be bass that haven't spawned yet, others that are in the middle of spawning, and still others that have been post-spawn for weeks. Depending on weather, water temperature, pH, the time of day and the availability of different kinds of food, you may

Bob Izumi hefts a largemouth caught on a plastic worm under a dock.

find bass on deep weed lines, in lily pads, under boat docks, off rocky points, in deep water, in shallow water, hovering over sunken islands or under a fallen-over tree only five yards offshore.

With other species, one or two methods are usually enough to produce a consistent limit, but with bass you can never seem to learn it all. One time they will be aggressive and ready to hit a crankbait or spinnerbait; another time they will be laid-back and passive, unlikely to react to anything short of a jig fluttered persistently in front of their noses. Fast retrieves, slow presentations, topwater lures, deep-divers—fishing for bass, you can be sure that sooner or later you'll have to use every item in your bag of tricks.

Inch-for-inch and pound-for-pound, I'm convinced nothing that swims offers quite the same excitement or sport as these amazingly versatile fish.

HABITS AND HISTORY

In many ways, the largemouth and smallmouth are alike. Both are members of the sunfish family (*Centrarchidae*), which also includes the popular bluegills and pumpkinseeds, and both are associated in people's minds with summer and sun. Their shapes are roughly similar, and so are their basic bone structure and anatomy.

Both were originally river fish whose native ranges were limited to the eastern half of the United States and the southeastern part of Canada. But their fighting (and good eating) qualities are so great that they have been widely stocked. Today, the largemouth can be found in nearly every U.S. state, including Hawaii, and across southern Canada, from New Brunswick to Manitoba and parts of southern British Columbia. The smallmouth is represented throughout the eastern United States as far south as Georgia, and in Canada from Nova Scotia to Saskatchewan and in parts of B.C. In Canada, only

Largemouth distribution.

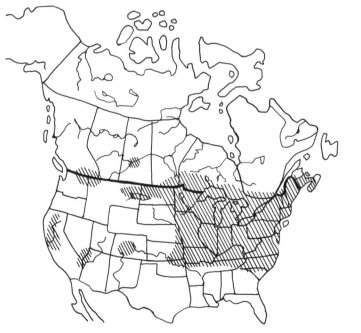

Smallmouth distribution.

Newfoundland, Alberta, the Yukon and the Northwest Territories are so unlucky as to have neither a
smallmouth nor a largemouth population.

Of course, Old Bucketmouth and his little
cousin start life like all other fish, hatching and
growing through the fry and fingerling stages in an
underwater world where it seems everything wants
to eat them. The young fish school above the circular spawning beds cleared by their parents on the
lake bottom. They are guarded by the male fish for
three weeks or more after hatching, but beyond this
short time they're on their own. Birds, animals and
other fish—even other bass—join the chase, trying to
gulp them down.

Only a tiny percentage of the thousands of fry
that hatch ever live to reach adulthood. As a result,
the survivors develop certain ingrained patterns.
Even big, aggressive adults ("Hawgs so ugly you can
hear 'em snort," as they say in Georgia) retain an
instinctive tendency to avoid signals—shadows on
the water, sudden movements, particular kinds of
splashes—that they associate with the predators they
fled as fingerlings. They shy away from open,
lighted areas, keeping under cover among weeds,
rocks, deadfalls and snags. If pike or muskie are
cruising the open waters, bass will stick especially
close to shelter. Only in lakes with no pike or muskie
do bass range regularly beyond the edges of weed
lines or rockfalls.

Bass, in fact, prefer cover even when they
themselves are doing the hunting. Contrary to the
long, sleek pike, whose streamlining makes it the
cheeta of the underwater world, a bass's body is
comparatively short and blunt—highly maneuvera-
ble, but not really built for speed. Bass prefer to hide
in ambush, then pounce on their prey in a sudden,
short rush. You can see them sometimes in the
weeds, waiting and watching, their bodies completely concealed among the leaves and stems with

Largemouth waiting in ambush for its prey.

only the tips of their noses poking out.

Those bass that do live to adulthood can thank a number of factors besides the availability of cover, among them a good sense of sight, of hearing and of smell.

A bass's vision is surprisingly sharp, much better than any fisherman's. A bass is five times more sensitive to light than a human, and can see in water that looks as opaque to us as a mud cocktail. Its eyes are located so that it can see simultaneously ahead, to the sides, behind and even up and down. Research shows that on calm days, especially in shallow water, a bass can also spot movement above water level, such as an angler walking down to the shore. Last but not least, bass also seem to be able to distinguish a wide range of colors—a good thing to keep in mind when choosing your arsenal of lures.

However, like most creatures, including people, they don't distinguish colors well at night, when simple light and shadow are the leading visual factors. After dark, a fish looking up toward the surface will distinguish only the dark silhouette of your lure against the lighter background. Color is thus of no consequence in night fishing.

As for the acuteness of the bass's sense of smell and hearing, I've seen graphic proof. Several times, I've caught adult bass that were blind in one or both eyes from scarring or cataracts. These fish were a bit thinner than their sighted counterparts, but they were a long way from starving to death. Obviously, they'd been foraging for food for quite a while without being able to see a thing.

Bass, in fact, come equipped with two sets of sound-detecting systems: an inner ear hidden under the skin on each side of the fish's head, and a series of sensors spotted along the lateral line on both sides of the body. The inner ear is used to detect sound vibrations that travel through the water from 25 feet or more away, while the lateral line hearing organs pick up soundwaves from sources nearer-by. Sound travels faster through water than through air, and since the bass's sensors are far keener than our ears, an alert fish doesn't miss much of what happens in the sound department. The lateral line is so sensitive that a bass can pinpoint the exact location of even a tiny sound anywhere within a 20-foot radius of its body.

Drop a metal tackle box or an oar in the bottom of an aluminum boat and every fish within 50 yards will dart away. To them, it sounds as if you're trying to hit a submarine with a depth charge.

Of course, there are some sounds fish like. Largemouth in shallow water like the light "plop" of a lure hitting the water—a plastic worm flipped softly next to a lily pad, for example. Small, non-aggressive-sounding noises actually attract bass, as do the whirring and splashing of topwater buzzbaits, which seem to irritate them into striking.

Obviously, the sound of a big outboard motor, especially one towing a pair of water skiers behind it, will spook fish. Its vibrations are completely foreign to the underwater environment. So are splashing oars turning in creaky oarlocks and clumsily-wielded canoe paddles slapping the water. Strangely, however, the hum of an electric trolling motor doesn't seem to bother fish as much. Those who have investigated the phenomenon seem to think that the currents created by an electric motor are different than those produced by large outboards or oars. Bass seem to perceive them as less threatening than other disturbances.

This is the reason behind the familiar combination of power sources used by pros on the bass tournament circuit: a big, 150 or more horsepower gasoline outboard to move the bass boat quickly from one honey hole to another, and a small, bow-mounted electric motor for maneuvering quietly once the chosen spot is reached and the outboard has been shut off.

Finally, we come to the bass's sense of smell— a part of the fishing equation that until recently was ignored by all but the canniest hog-hunters. It's impossible to explain why it was ignored. Outdoorsmen have always known that animals have a keen sense of smell. So why not fish? Why should a hunter know enough not to approach game from upwind, or to use musk to hide the human scent while he's sitting on a deer stand, but a fisherman— often the same man—never give scent a thought on the water?

We'll probably never know. But, as the burgeoning popularity of commercial scent baits proves, the fishing fraternity has at last caught on and is making up for lost time.

In the bass's case, it's none too soon. The sense of smell is probably the most highly developed of all of the bass's senses, and failure to pay attention to it puts any fisherman at a serious disadvantage. The two nostrils on either side of its head are discriminating enough to put a bloodhound to shame. Here's

BIG JAWS AND LITTLE JAWS

Landing Old Bucketmouth.

how Al and Ron Lindner's *In-Fisherman* team described it in their study of bass:

Scientific experiments conducted on coho and chinook salmon demonstrated that these fish could detect less than two hundredths of a drop of seal (a natural predator) extract in a 23,000-gallon swimming pool. Now that's a sensitive sniffer. No formal studies have been conducted on bass, and their noses may not be quite so sensitive as a salmon's, but the fact that bass can locate prey in murky water and at night tells us they, too, have a keen sense of smell.

The internal scent-detecting organs of fish, to which their nostrils channel odors, are made up of groups of leaf-shaped folds. Scientists haven't proven it yet, but they suspect that the more folds there are, the better the fish's sense of smell operates. Because the number of scent folds apparently increases with age, this could mean that, the older and larger a lunker bass is, the better its smeller works.

The scent baits manufactured commercially employ three types of odor-producing chemicals: amino acids, pheromones and cover-up compounds such as anise. Anise, or licorice scent, does nothing more than hide the human odor. Amino acids, however, are the actual chemical markers that identify each species, and are detectable by other species. For example, the human smell is the amino acid L-serine. Animals and fish alike seem to find this the most offensive odor imaginable. To them, we reek like old socks! Pheromones, on the other hand, are hormone-like chemicals that transmit messages from one member of the species to another. The strongest of all scents, they advertise such things as readiness to mate, or a feeling of panic after serious injury.

It doesn't take much of any of these kinds of scent to alert a bass, and turn it on or off according to what the scent conveys. For instance, if a fisherman fuels up an outboard, splashing gasoline or oil all over his hands, then picks up a crankbait and ties it on his line, chances are he'll be giving fish a double dose of offensive odors: a mixture of L-serine and the gasoline or oil smell. Dropping so tainted a lure into the water will probably have the same effect on fish as dropping a stinkbomb would have on a crowd of Parisian perfume-testers. Another example: catching a northern pike, which eats bass, and then throwing the same lure that caught the pike into a school of smallmouths is like sending those fish the signal, "Don't eat me, stay away!"

By the same token, dousing the same lure with a commercial preparation like essence of crayfish could ring Little Jaws's dinner bell, and provoke him into striking.

Offensive odors to a bass, such as gas, outboard motor oil and sunscreen, can be transferred from your hands to a lure. To eliminate these odors from your hands, wash with no-scent soap designed especially for fishermen or with plain old dish detergent.

Rocky Crawford holds a largemouth in his right hand and a smallmouth in his left. The largemouth was caught on a weedless jig and pig under floating weeds and the smallmouth on a jig in submerged rocks.

WEATHER OR NOT

Both largemouth and smallmouth are also influenced by the weather, particularly by the passage of cold fronts and, on a larger scale, by changes of season. Fish are cold-blooded, like reptiles, and thus cannot regulate their own body temperature. Unlike mammals, which maintain a constant temperature regardless of how hot or cold it is around them, the body temperatures of fish rise or fall according to the temperature of the water they swim in. If the water is warm, so are the fish, and their activity increases accordingly. If the water temperature drops, the fish cool off too, not only in temperature but also in terms of activity. A school of bass that would fight for your bubble gum if you spat it overboard on a warm day, will slow right down and ignore even the tastiest morsels after a cold front has passed through.

Bass can survive in temperatures ranging from as low as 33°F (.6°C) to 90°F (32°C), but seem to function best in or around the 70s. According to the authoritative *Freshwater Fishes of Canada*, smallmouth bass generally spawn in water temperatures from 55° to 68°F (13° to 20°C), and largemouth from 62° to 65°F (17° to 18°C).

Yet another factor that affects bass behavior is the pH, or acidity/alkalinity of the water they live in. On the pH scale, which runs from 0 to 14, the number 7 is neutral. Anything above 7 is basic; anything below it is acidic. For example, pure distilled water has a pH of 7, while vinegar has a pH of 2.5 and an alkaline substance such as baking soda has a pH of 8.5. Each change of one unit represents a change in concentration ten times that of the number nearest it.

The pH of a lake is important to fish because it can alter both the chemical content of the water and the ability of their bodies to perform certain functions. For example, at low (or acidic) pH levels, fish find it tougher to absorb oxygen through their gills, to maintain the correct salinity level in their blood and to regulate their calcium intake. If the pH drops far enough, spawning will be adversely affected, along with the survival rate of those fry that are produced. Toxic aluminum, dissolved from the soil, may concentrate in the water and eventually kill the adult fish. This is one of the reasons why the problem of acid rain is so serious: if our lakes and streams become too acidic, we may lose not only our bass, but all of our game fish.

Bass will leave an area—or if they're trapped in it, die—if the pH of the water falls below roughly 6.8 or climbs much higher than 8.5. They can survive fairly well anywhere between those two extremes, but seem to function best in a pH range of 7.5 to 7.9, depending on a combination of water temperature and other factors. This range could be described as the bass's pH comfort zone, and they'll put up with a great deal to stay in it. Faced with the choice of staying in water with a more pleasant temperature and higher oxygen content but with a low pH, or moving to a spot where the temperature is colder and oxygen scarcer but with a pH in the comfort zone, bass will go for the right pH.

Obviously, if you're trying to locate bass, pH is a key element and use of a pH meter to read a lake makes a lot of sense.

The pH of different areas of a lake or river changes with the temperature, rising when it gets warmer and falling when it gets chilly. In fact, some scientists believe it is the rise in pH in the shallow waters near shore that draws bass in to spawn in the spring, rather than the actual rise in temperature itself.

So strong is the influence of pH on bass behavior that some scientists, and many fishermen, believe a pH meter can be used to pinpoint the depth at which bass may be schooled on a given day. The idea is to find the water depth at which the pH changes sharply. If a pH probe is lowered and every foot or so the pH changes only slightly—then, at six feet it suddenly jumps from 7.1 to 8.1—the level where the major change occurs is where the fish should be.

I wouldn't go so far as to say that this method works 100 percent of the time, but I will say that I know pH affects bass. I've seen it myself in tournaments. Once, my partner and I were fishing for largemouth on riprap, using spinnerbaits and plastic worms. We caught only a few fish, and those were thin and sickly-looking. My brother Wayne and his partner were fishing another area—identical to ours in every way but pH—and they pulled in fat, healthy fish after fat, healthy fish using the same baits and same methods. I'm convinced pH was the key to that situation. The water where my partner and I were fishing was too acid for healthy fish and only held runts.

The amount of oxygen in the water can also affect fish. In the 1970s, oxygen level meters were popular among the more technically minded anglers. The meters proved somewhat unreliable, though, and when it was found that pH was much more important, they went out of favor. I haven't seen one on the market in quite a while. In general, water with a high oxygen content is better for game fish, and only coarse fish, such as carp, do well in low-oxygen conditions. The presence of fresh, growing weeds, which take in carbon dioxide and give out oxygen, makes water more hospitable to fish. Large amounts of dead, rotting vegetation, on the other hand, use up oxygen and make the area less attractive to game fish.

Temperature, pH, early conditioning, the availability of cover and food—all these things affect bass behavior. So do even more subtle influences, from tiny changes in salinity (a rise in salinity can affect fish like a tonic, boosting their metabolism and activity) to individual differences in bass personality.

It's true. Fish seem to have personalities—or at least a set of quirks so variable I can't describe them with any other word. The most noticeable trait is aggressiveness, or the lack of it. Some bass just seem to be more vicious or ornery than others. They'll strike at anything, and keep striking even after being caught and released by a fisherman. Wayne caught the same bass six times over a two-year period. It was a big old thing with a distinctive, L-shaped scar, and Wayne kept catching it on the same rock pile. After a while, he thought maybe we should name it and I said, "Yeah, call it Stupid." But it wasn't so much stupid as super-aggressive. Other fish are just plain greedy. I know of rock bass that have scooped up two baits at the same time, first sucking in one fisherman's worm and then hitting another one nearby. Two lines, two hooks and two fishermen pulling in the same fish!

Other bass will strike at a lure, get caught and released, and never hit an artificial bait again in their lives. Still others won't even hit that first time. Are they less aggressive, more discriminating or just smarter? I don't know, but for sure they're not a bunch of fish/robots, all stamped out of the same mold and acting alike. They're individuals.

Each group of fish acts differently, as well.

Bob with a smallie caught on a deep-diving crayfish imitation crankbait on boulder-strewn bottom.

Some move around a lake, covering several acres of territory, while others tend to home in on their own "turf," favoring a particular range over all the others. Some fish like to travel in large schools, others prefer small groups, and still others go off alone, like the old African rogue elephant. Predicting where they might be at a given moment isn't a matter of science, but of art.

Of course, as numerous as their similarities are, the largemouth and smallmouth are still separate species, and their differences can be crucial to a basser in hot pursuit. Let's take a look at some of them.

Largemouth bass.

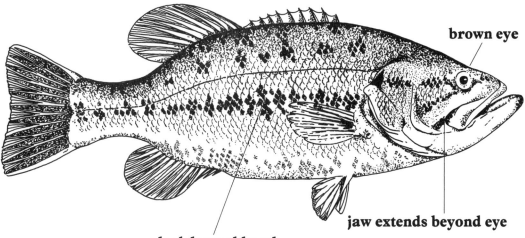

brown eye

jaw extends beyond eye

dark lateral band

THE LARGEMOUTH

Mister Big Jaws, as its name indicates, has a big mouth. The maxillary, or upper jawbone, runs back past the eye in adults, while the lower jaw sticks out beyond the snout, making a wide gape—wide enough for a frog or any hapless smaller fish that comes within range to disappear into forever.

The largemouth is a big fish in other ways, as well. The largest specimen on record, caught in Montgomery Lake, Georgia, in 1932, weighed in at 22 pounds, 4 ounces and measured 32½ inches in length. In the land of the maple leaf, where the largemouth is sometimes called a green bass by English-speakers and *achigan à grande bouche* by French, the record catch was hooked on Stoney Lake, near Peterborough, Ontario, in 1948. Its weight—14 pounds, 2 ounces—topped many northern U.S. state records.

That's a lot of fish in anybody's book.

It's a handsome one, too, deep-bodied, with rich olive-green back and sides and cream-white undersides (both the largemouth and smallmouth, however, change coloration slightly to match their surroundings, turning more tan over sand, green in murky water, etc.). Its eyes are brown, and a wide, black lateral band is often visible running from snout to tail. And, finally, it's powerful, swimming and striking with heavy authority.

The largemouth has been stocked in a variety of habitats, including deep, rocky reservoirs, and has proven capable of adapting to almost any conditions. But in natural lakes and streams, this species' preferred turf is shallow water, warmed by the sun. With the exception of many U.S. reservoirs, catching Old Bigmouth in anything deeper than 20 feet of water is a relatively rare event.

Weeds and soft bottom—mud or soft sand—are its favorite cover, along with stumps, snags and deadfalls. Deep-water weeds—milfoil and pondweed—are ideal cover for many fish and occasionally for the largemouth as well, but the largemouth is more often found among emergent plants such as water lilies, cattails or coontail, either near shore or on shallow offshore weed flats.

Some experienced anglers believe Big Jaws does well in fairly cool waters, but scientists say it thrives best in water from 79.8° to 81.9°F (26.6° to 27.7°C). Largemouth, like other game fish, have more trouble surviving in low-oxygen conditions, such as waters where significant amounts of decomposing vegetation are present.

Spawning times for bass can vary widely from lake to lake, but in the same lake, largemouth will usually spawn slightly sooner than smallmouth. This, as the authors of *Freshwater Fishes of Canada* explain, is "because the shallower, protected spawning sites in quiet bays, among emergent vegetation, warm to the optimum temperature sooner than do the deeper, rockier sites used by the smallmouth." Also, as a general rule, spawning will take place earlier in the northwest corner of a lake, which tends to get more sun. The round, saucer-like nesting beds are swept clear on the lake bottom by the male fish, who fan away vegetation and debris with their fins. Located in water two to four feet deep and averaging from two to three feet in diameter (sometimes more), these beds are surprisingly symmetrical.

The female scatters eggs over the bed, right out to the edges, and the male guards them and the fry that hatch with fierce territoriality. Spawning and guarding the nest take a lot out of these fish, and they are often thin and a bit ragged-looking when it's over. Post-spawn fish may be a bit lethargic until they recover and resume active hunting and feeding.

When lunchtime does roll around, the largemouth likes fresh meat, especially other fish. Between 50 and 90 percent of its diet consists of small fish and, being a remorseless cannibal (much more so than the smallmouth), this often includes the young of its own species. That big buck, battling to keep other fish away from its spawning bed, probably has more trouble with other largemouth than with any other species. One study reported that as much as 10 percent of the food of largemouth eight inches or more in length is the fry of its own species. Another 10 to 40 percent of Mr. Big Jaws's dinner menu is comprised of frogs, worms, crayfish and large insect nymphs.

Although it grows bigger on this fare than its smallmouth cousin—and can feel like a monster when you've got it on your line—our friend Hugechops isn't quite the same kind of scrapper as the smallie. Most of its resistance seems to go on underwater, without the tailwalking and other spectacular surface acrobatics for which its relative is famous.

As if to make up for this comparative calm, however, the largemouth is more active in winter than the smallmouth, moving to the bottom in deeper water, where it is sometimes taken by ice fishermen.

Smallmouth bass.

red or orange eye

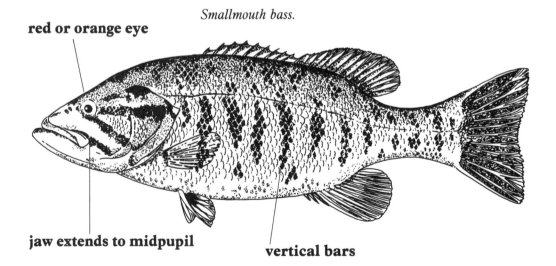

jaw extends to midpupil

vertical bars

THE SMALLMOUTH

The appetite of the smallmouth is no less voracious than that of its larger relative, but—again as

the name indicates—the business end of that appetite is smaller. The upper jawbone of Little Jaws
extends just to, but not beyond, the middle of the
eye. The eye itself is usually red or orange (in
contrast to the largemouth's brown), and the dark
lateral band characteristic of the largemouth is
absent.

The back and sides of the smallmouth are
usually brown to olive green, the undersides cream
to milk-white, and, instead of a lateral band, its sides
are marked with a series of dark brown to black
vertical stripes. The depth of the smallmouth's col-
oring changes with its surroundings, and the stripes
may be more pronounced in one type of cover than
in another. But the stripes are, nevertheless, the
most obvious and characteristic identifier of the
species.

The world's record size smallmouth bass was
caught in Dale Hollow Lake, Kentucky, in 1955. It
weighed 11 pounds, 15 ounces and measured 27
inches in length. In Canada, the largest smallmouth
caught appears to be one pulled out of Birchbark
Lake, near Kinmount, Ontario, in 1954, which
weighed 9 pounds, 13 ounces.

Like the largemouth, the smallmouth has been
widely stocked and has managed to adapt to a variety of habitats. In general, however, the smallie is a
deeper water fish. While a school of largemouths
may happily pass half the summer on a weed flat no
more than four feet deep, smallmouths are far more
likely to congregate at depths of fifteen feet or
more—especially when the spawning period is over
and the hot dog-days of July and August have
arrived.

Smallmouths are rarely found in really thick
weeds, especially not the shore-hugging cattails
and water lilies the largemouth loves. They prefer
the open areas—boulder slopes, sandbars, sunken
islands and, above all, rocks. In fact, if the name

hadn't already been taken by its little panfish relative, rock bass wouldn't have been a bad name for the smallmouth. Smallies love rocks, and anything that resembles rock, such as concrete breakwalls, riprap and the like.

Smallmouths prefer rocks to weeds.

The reason for their attachment to rock is no mystery, nor is it some odd quirk of nature without apparent explanation. It's literally a matter of taste. The favorite food of the smallmouth bass is that familiar freshwater cousin of the lobster—the crayfish. And crayfish are found in greatest abundance among rocks. Biologists who have studied the stomach contents of smallmouths for years, weighing them on delicate scales and recording the results in carefully kept notebooks, say that crayfish make up from 60 to 90 percent of the average smallmouth's diet. In fact, if a constant, unending supply of these little lobster look-alikes was available, the typical smallmouth probably wouldn't eat anything else.

Unfortunately for Little Jaws, crayfish aren't always on the menu, and sometimes it has to make do with substitutes. Roughly ten percent of the

Wayne Izumi caught this smallmouth on a spinnerbait in a weed flat.

smallmouth diet thus consists of fish, with a few frogs, tadpoles, insects and fish eggs thrown in for balance.

Smallmouths prefer not only deeper, more open waters than largemouths, but cooler ones as well. The optimum water temperature range for smallmouths is between 68.5° and 70.3°F (20.3° and 21.3°C). It is this preference for deeper, cooler waters that accounts in part for the smallmouth's later spawning period. It takes longer for deep water to warm up to the ideal spawning temperatures of between 55° and 68°F (13° and 20°C) than it does for shallower areas.

Thus, in a given lake, smallmouths may spawn as much as three weeks to one month later than largemouths. Their beds, slightly smaller and less carefully cleaned than those of the largemouth, range from one to six feet in diameter and may be cleared in water from two to twenty feet deep. Unlike the largemouth, which scatters its eggs all over the spawning bed, the smallmouth female generally deposits its eggs toward the center of the nest. As with the largemouth, the male smallmouth assumes the duty of guarding the eggs and the young for periods of one to three weeks after they hatch.

In winter, smallmouths are much less active than largemouths. They school near the bottom of frozen lakes, eat very little and—compared to their summer patterns—hardly move from dawn to dusk. It's a rare event indeed for an ice fisherman to catch a smallmouth. Not until lake waters reach at least a minimum temperature of 47°F (8.5°C) do the smallies resume active feeding.

Unlike the largemouth, which tends to prefer quieter waters with relatively little current, the smallmouth favors flowing water, stirred either by currents or wave action.

PARASITES AND PREDATORS

Like all wild creatures, both the largemouth and smallmouth are plagued by parasites, most of which are harmless to man. The smallmouth is frequently attacked by the bass tapeworm (*Proteocephalus ambloplitis*), which can cause sterility in fish, and by both black spot and yellow grubs, which are visually repellent to look at but which cause no physical harm to humans when the infested fish are cooked before eating.

The most important natural enemies of adult bass are the pike and muskie and, of course, man. The growing popularity of catch-and-release fishing—a conservation measure of obvious value in areas where fishing pressure is unusually heavy and where lunkers are becoming increasingly rare—may someday change the equation. But, as of today, bass (especially smallmouth) are among the top five game fish in Canada, and largemouth are the number one game fish in the United States. They haven't been harvested commercially in Canada since the mid-1930s, but bass are one of the mainstays of the present tourist and sport fishing industries here and in the United States.

In short, I'm not alone. Thousands of other fishermen and women across North America agree: bass are the kings of freshwater sport fishing, and Big Jaws and Little Jaws are kings among the kings.

TWO

BEST BASS TACKLE

If you work at it hard enough, you can catch fish with a tree branch, a piece of string and a safety pin. But unless you're a survivalist trying to prove you can live off the land, that's doing it the hard way. Tackle made specifically for the purpose works much better and, in the case of bass, equipment designed with this particular family of fish in mind works best of all.

A fly rod, for example, is an excellent tool for catching trout and salmon, and I know several anglers who also use one to fish for pike. In a few circumstances you can catch bass on a fly rod, too, and some bassers even do it deliberately for fun and a change of pace, but it sure wouldn't make the best all-around pole for bass. What good is a dry fly flicked on top of the water if you're trying to attract a school of smallmouth suspended on rocks 25 feet deep? If you're after largemouth, a long, whippy fly rod isn't exactly the best implement for horsing lunkers through thick weeds and lily pad stems, either. If bass are your quarry, spinning or bait-casting equipment is the best choice for the job.

Each of these two types of tackle has its own set of drawbacks and advantages, but before getting into them, let's deal with some aspects of tackle that hold true for both.

A typical assortment of tournament rods and reels in a bass boat.

BALANCED BUDGET, BALANCED TACKLE

Cost is a key factor. Just as a professional auto mechanic who uses tools every day won't hesitate to buy the best equipment on the market, so a professional fisherman may spend thousands of dollars a year on his tackle. I make my living as a fisherman and depend on high-quality equipment to give me a competitive edge in tournaments. But not every do-it-yourselfer who does an occasional home car repair needs a complete set of chrome-molybdenum socket wrenches—nor does every weekend fisherman need the kind of tackle my brother Wayne and I take for granted. Your choice of rod and reel combinations should be dictated by how much fishing you actually plan to do and how specialized you want to become.

If you only get down to the lake once or twice a month during the summer, you can buy an adequate rod and reel combination, including line and a few lures, for under $100. If you're a more serious angler who considers catching bass an essential part of life, you can spend more than $100 for the reel alone. In fact, you'll probably end up buying several rods and reels to meet various situations. I generally have anywhere from six to eight rods, each with its own reel, in the boat when I'm on the water. These include both spinning and bait–casting outfits, and each is matched according to weight and action to be of maximum value in a specific instance.

There are three basic types of rod action—light, medium and heavy—and you can test for them yourself in the tackle shop. Some people do it by grabbing the handle and holding the rod at arm's length, with the tip against the wall, then applying pressure. If the rod bends only a tiny bit right at the tip, its action is heavy; if it bends about a third of the way back from the tip, it's a medium-action rod, and if it bends gradually along its whole length, you've got a light-action rod. If you bend it too hard and it snaps, you've got a bill to pay. Personally, I don't do it that way. It seems a lot more natural to me just to tie on a lure or practice plug, maybe a ¼-ounce plug, reel it up tight to the rod tip and see where it bends the rod and how the action feels in your hand.

When applied to reels, the terms *light*, *medium* and *heavy* (or *medium-light*, *medium-heavy* and all of the other gradations introduced lately by manufacturers) refer to the weight of line the reel is designed to handle. A heavy bait-casting reel for muskie, for example, is designed to hold 20-, 30- or even 40-pound test line. A medium casting reel would carry anything from 8- to 20-pound test and a medium spinning reel from 6 to 12.

To be most effective, tackle should be balanced. Each item—rod, reel, line and lure—should complement the others and match the situation in which it is likely to be used. A "wet noodle" light-action steelhead rod, for instance, would be useless against a 40-pound muskie, and the kind of heavy-action reel designed for big fish would look ridiculous on such a rod. A big muskie crankbait would feel like a lead brick on the end of it. Trying to use a stubby, heavy-action rod made for pulling large-mouths through lily pad stems to cast a little ¹⁄₁₆-ounce spinner tied to a feather-light line would be equally silly. If you're using a light lure and light line, then a light reel and light- to medium-action rod are needed. If you're throwing heavy crankbaits or spoons with heavy line, a heavier reel and stiffer rod are appropriate.

Matching each of these components requires a certain amount of personal judgement, and the choices aren't always obvious. I'll note some of my general preferences shortly, and go into more detail in later chapters when we look at various fishing situations.

Also important considerations when choosing a rod and reel are the materials and methods used to

Heavy, medium and light rod action.

make them. Thirty years ago, rods were made of spring steel or split bamboo, and reels of steel. Then fiberglass rods and plastic reels came in, and finally today's graphite, titanium, boron and combination equipment arrived on the market.

Of course, steel rods have gone the way of the 78 rpm record, and split bamboo is used almost exclusively today to build handmade fly rods. Fiberglass is still very popular, and a glass rod can be an economical investment for someone who doesn't have much money to spend and does only a modest amount of fishing.

But if you're serious about angling—and if you chase bass very long you'll get serious—I recommend spending $20 or $30 more for the extra sensitivity of a graphite rod. By the same token, a medium-priced ($25 to $35) metal spinning reel will likely be more than adequate for the weekend angler, but a serious fisherman who plans on spending many hours on the water will appreciate the combination of strength and light weight of a graphite reel. After hundreds of casts, even weights measured in ounces begin to take their toll in the form of a stiff wrist.

So much has been made of the fabulous virtues of graphite that it would probably be useful to go into a little detail here, and dispel some myths. Graphite is an excellent rod-making material, but it won't perform miracles or do your fishing for you. Like any other fiber used to construct rod shafts, it has its good and bad points, and the ultimate quality of the product made with it has more to do with how the manufacturer puts it together than how "pure" it is.

What makes graphite useful is that it is both light and stiff. Unlike glass, which is a relatively heavy and weakly bound combination of several chemical elements, graphite is pure crystal carbon—a lightweight element with an exceptionally strong

A pistol grip bait-casting rod, two spinning rods and a long-handled bait-casting rod, all made of boron-reinforced graphite.

internal bond. That bond provides the kind of stiffness that lets an angler feel the slightest touch of a nibbling fish, and also produces the "damping down" effect that minimizes vibration along the rod shaft after a cast, increasing accuracy. On the minus side, graphite is more brittle than glass. Unless manufacturers compensate for this quality by using special fiber weaves or combining the graphite with other materials, it can lead to easier breakage.

Graphite rods can be made with fiber "roving" (strands of uneven lengths twisted into loose braids), with woven fabric (graphite threads crisscrossing one another) or with uni-directional tape (flat strips of thousands of parallel graphite fibers held together with epoxy). Roving is the cheapest form of graphite fiber and is usually used in fiberglass combination rods—sometimes as a mere advertising gimmick to allow the maker to claim his rod is "graphite." Better-quality rods generally use fabric or tape, or a combination of both, and the very best use only "high-modulus" fibers, manufactured via special heat and pressure processes to impart above-average strength and flexibility.

The relative merits and demerits of each kind of graphite fiber and rod design could fill a book by themselves. Basically, however, you get what you pay for. The best graphite rods have better warranties, feel good in your hand and cost more. If you want a graphite, buy it at a reputable tackle shop, insist on a warranty and use common sense when you look at the price tag.

A medium-weight graphite-titanium spinning reel and rod.

SPINNING TACKLE

Since the 1950s, when they began to make their way from France and Britain (where they'd been popular for years) to North America, spinning rods and reels have grown in popularity until, today, they are probably preferred by more Canadian and American anglers than any other type of tackle. Unlike bait-casting reels, afflicted as they are by that familiar and frustrating plague, the backlash (on the tournament circuit we call it a "professional overrun"), spinning reels don't require an "educated thumb" to operate. Even the greenest beginner can quickly learn to use one, lobbing crankbaits and spinners after a day's practice with almost as much ease as if he'd been doing it for years. The reason for this is that line plays off the front-facing spinning reel spool in wide loops, like the circular spray of grass clippings thrown off by the blades of a rotary power mower. Because the spool itself stays stationary (only the bale turns), there is no time lag between the rate of spool rotation and the rate at which each loop drops away. In contrast, a bait-casting reel revolves horizontally, like the blades of an old-fashioned reel-type lawnmower, with the spool axle itself turning. During a cast, if the fisherman doesn't use thumb pressure to slow its speed of rotation, the spool may revolve faster than the line can peel off. Presto: a bird's nest.

Of course, through years of practice, I have developed an educated thumb and—as I'll explain shortly—if I could only take one rod and reel bassing I'd choose a bait-casting outfit. But due to their ease of handling and because they are also practical for many non-bass species, spinning outfits are a frequent general-purpose choice of beginning bassers with modest tackle-buying budgets. They also tend to be superior in situations where lighter line—four- to eight-pound test—is being used. I frequently employ a spinning rod with light line fishing for smallmouths because the line seems to flow better off the stationary spool.

I find several rod/reel combinations valuable. However, narrowing it down to a single all-around spinning combination that would work for both largemouth and smallmouth, I'd choose a six-foot-long, medium-action graphite rod. I prefer a medium-action for an all-around rod because the first third of the rod's length is flexible enough to provide a sensitive touch for detecting nibbles, feeling the lure's action and cushioning the shock of a hard-fighting fish's movements, while the remaining two-thirds of the rod shaft is stiff enough to provide the backbone for a good hook-set. As for the reel, I'd go for a medium-weight one designed to handle six- to twelve-pound test line. If you have the extra money, I'd definitely recommend a graphite or graphite/titanium reel for the sake of lightness. This spinning rod and reel combination won't

◄ Some manufacturers virtually tie their rods in knots to prove their strength. However, when shopping for a rod, strength is not as important as sensitivity, action and balance.

be perfect for every fishing situation, but it will handle quite a few of them well and the others at least adequately.

At the tackle shop, you'll find a confusing array of reels, some of them looking as if they had been designed for use in outer space rather than on a lake. High-tech has come to fishing and, if you want, you can even buy a bait-casting reel with a digital read-out micro-computer system whose screen tells you the length of line that went out on your cast, the depth at which your lure is running and the speed of your retrieve. Some spinning reels are almost as complicated, and are loaded with as many push buttons and calibrated dials as an expensive camera.

Basically though, there are only a couple of things you really have to think about. First, be sure the crank handle is on the side that fits you; for spinning reels, which are designed to hang under the rod, this will be on the left if you're right-handed, or on the right if you're a southpaw. There are some people who prefer to cast with their weak hand and crank the reel with their strong hand, especially when they're fighting a big fish whose weight makes cranking difficult. But most people like to cast with the hand that gives them the greatest control and crank the lure in with the other. Pick a reel with fast-retrieve gearing for maximum control.

Second, examine the drag system. For years the drag control on spinning rods was set by adjusting a wing nut on the front of the reel spool, tightening the nut clockwise to increase the drag and backing it off to decrease it. You judged how heavy you'd set your drag by pulling out the line and feeling its resistance. More recently, reels have been developed with precisely calibrated drag controls mounted at the back of the reel, behind the crank handle. The numbered settings on rear-drag models permit much more accurate adjustments. Particularly handy is the "fighting drag" system introduced by Shimano in 1985. This type of rear drag allows you to pre-set your drag at two different levels, one for hook-setting and one for fighting. A left/right lever control allows you to switch from one setting to another without looking at the numbers on the dial.

Because they are more complex, rear-drag models as a rule cost a bit more than front-drag ones. There are, of course, anglers who swear by the front-drag system—and swear at rear-drag models—

The rear-drag control on a spinning reel permits precision adjustment.

The front control drag system on a spinning reel is still common.

A selection of long-handled bait-casting outfits.

claiming rear-drag reels don't stand up to hard wear when fighting big fish. I disagree totally with that. Unless you're salt-water fishing, or are fighting ten-pound bass on one-pound test line, a well-constructed rear-drag reel made by a reputable manufacturer will do just fine. I use one myself for steelhead and have had nothing but good results. No bass is ever going to wear out your reel. The only question to consider is whether the greater precision of rear-drag models is important enough to you to warrant the extra expense.

Finally, consider the quality of design and materials used in the reel you select. Steer clear of cheap plastic and white metal reels, which crack and break too easily. If your budget allows, pick a reel whose crank turns on ball bearings, rather than bushings. The best reels are made with stainless steel ball bearings and brass or stainless steel gears and will continue to turn smoothly for years.

BAIT-CASTING TACKLE

The old, reliable bait-casting rod has been around much longer than spinning tackle, and continued to be the preferred type of equipment in North America long after the spinning rod had taken Europe by storm. Not until the 1960s and 70s, when spinning tackle really caught on in both Canada and the United States, was the supremacy of bait casting threatened. Today, this traditional method of fishing is making a comeback—particularly among bass fishermen.

A level-wind bait-casting reel.

A side view of a level-wind bait-casting reel showing its modern low-profile teardrop shape designed for easy gripping.

Long-handled bait-casting rods have become very common among tournament anglers in particular. They use them for two-handed casting with heavy lures or in all-day casting situations. More distance when casting and better leverage, fighting and handling of bass can be achieved with this new addition to a basser's arsenal.

It never had to make a comeback with me, because I never quit using it. There's no question in my mind that a bait-casting rod is the best tool to use on largemouth, especially if you're fishing in thick weeds or near heavy, overhanging brush along a shoreline. In this kind of situation, I like a comfortable, pistol-grip-style bait-casting rod between five feet, six inches and six feet long, with a good, thick butt and fairly heavy action. For a reel, I'd choose a medium-weight model designed for eight- to twenty-pound test line, teardrop-shaped for easy palming.

With this kind of outfit, you can handle just about any largemouth situation. The stiffness of the rod gives you the power you need for a good hook-set and the strength to rip through those weeds. With a relatively short, pistol-grip rod you can side-cast, cast underhand beneath overhanging branches and, in general, get into all those tight places where lunkers like to hide.

Bait-casting equipment also seems to work best for flipping, although here I use a longer (though still heavy-action) rod—seven to seven and a half feet. This gives the extra leverage needed for longer flips. If you plan on fishing mostly for largemouths and like flipping, you'll find it worthwhile to invest in a specially designed flipping reel. The gears on this type of reel are built to give a high power ratio, rather than for high-speed retrieves, and include other features, such as controls that minimize backlash when you strip line.

Other points to consider in choosing a bait-casting reel include anti-backlash features, drag and, of course, which side the crank handle is on (because bait-casting reels mount on top of the rod, facing up, a "right-handed" reel is one with the crank handle on the right, the opposite of a right-hander's spinning reel).

Competition from the backlash-proof spinning

A level-wind reel designed especially for flipping.

Bob shows a selection of bait-casting rods and reels in his right hand and spinning rods and reels in his left hand.

◄ Bait-casting reels require a bit more maintenance than spinning reels. They have more exposed and moving parts which require oil and some grease. I would recommend oiling your bait-casting reel at least once a week under heavy use.

reel prompted bait-casting tackle manufacturers to look for ways to prevent line tangles. A variety of spool brake weights have been used to regulate the speed at which the spool turns, but the most significant—and successful—innovation has been the so-called mag reel. This type of reel, as its name suggests, employs magnets to control spool speed. The magnets are mounted near the metal spool, their distance from it—and hence their attracting power—regulated by a dial on the side of the reel casing. The dial can be set so that the higher the rpm's of the spool, the closer the magnets move and the stronger their attracting force. This keeps the spool from turning too fast for the line. Those irritating professional overruns aren't totally eliminated, but they are reduced to the point where they occur only rarely.

The drag on old-time bait-casting reels was set by a button control. It had only two positions, on and off; you could tell when the drag was on because the reel clicked as the line played out. Today's reels employ much more sophisticated drag systems. The best use star-wheel controls that, when turned, compress a series of drag washers. These apply pressure to the gear train and spool, permitting multiple drag settings.

Another point that sometimes confuses reel buyers, whether they're shopping for a bait-casting or spinning reel, is the line capacity of the spool. People seem to think they need hundreds of yards of line and that, if a spool won't hold that much, it isn't "big enough." I sometimes have to laugh in a tackle shop, when I hear somebody ask the salesman, "How much line will this reel hold?" The salesman will answer, "About one hundred fifty yards," and they say, "Oh, is that all?" How far does that person think he can cast?

Granted you need a lot of line if you're trolling for, say, lake trout, or using a downrigger to go after coho salmon. But for bass, at the very most you might need 75 yards. Ninety percent of the time you'll probably use only 25 yards of line, so the spool's capacity doesn't have to be very great. Of course, on a spinning reel the line will flow off the spool most smoothly during a cast if the spool is filled nearly to the edge of its lip (the optimum clearance varies according to the line thickness, $\frac{1}{16}$-inch for four-pound test line, $\frac{1}{8}$-inch for eight-pound, etc.). Some fishermen put on old line, electrical tape or rubber bands to fill in the space, then wind 100 yards or so of good line on top of that, until it reaches the right clearance. Most spools won't hold more than 200 to 300 yards of line, and some come with built-in adapters so you can only put on a certain maximum.

Most reels will hold more than enough line for bass fishing, so don't spend a lot of time worrying about capacity.

LINE AND TERMINAL TACKLE

The type of line you wind onto your reel is far more important than the amount. Clear, nylon monofilament is my own choice 50 percent of the time—especially when I'm after smallmouth in clear water. Where visibility is good, fish forage by sight and you want that line to be as close to invisible as possible, particularly when you're using slow-presentation baits that the fish have time to look at, such as jigs, plastic worms or live baits. Nylon also has superior strength, elasticity and abrasion resistance. Another recently developed line that I use the other 50 percent of the time is the Prime cofilament line. This has a polyester core with a nylon sheath and is much stiffer than regular nylon monofilament. As with graphite rods, this stiffness provides greater sensitivity in detecting nibbles and also seems to give a better hook-set.

I use colored or fluorescent lines in a minority

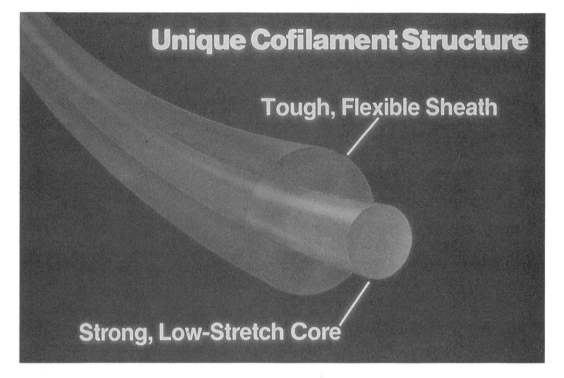

Unique Cofilament Structure

Tough, Flexible Sheath

Strong, Low-Stretch Core

Cofilament fishing line is more sensitive to strikes.

of situations, such as fishing for largemouths with plastic worms in thick cover. Here colored lines are useful because their color makes it easier for you to see them move when a fish takes the bait. With all the reeds and stems around, you don't have to worry as much about them spooking the fish, either.

Your choice of line weight should be determined by the kind of fishing you're doing, your rod and reel combination, the weight and action of your lure, the kind of cover the fish are in and the speed of your lure presentation. Obviously, with this many variables there are a lot of choices open, but picking the right line can be fairly straightforward if the principles involved are understood.

As already mentioned, there's no point using featherweight jigs or lures on a stiff, heavy-action rod, or heavy crankbaits and spoons on a whippy, light-action rod. The same is true in matching your line to your rod and lure. A heavy, 40-pound test line would completely ruin the action of a $1/16$-ounce jig, while a 4-pound test line might not have enough

Fishermen's knots: (A) Palomar knot; (B) uni-knot system; (C) improved clinch knot.

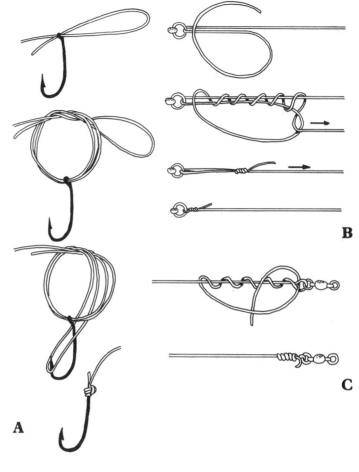

A

B

C

water resistance to slow the rate of sinking of a crankbait you're trying to work near the surface. A light line would also break too easily if you used it in heavy weeds or areas where a fish might tangle you up on underwater stumps or wind you around a rock. A lighter, less-visible line is an advantage jigging for smallmouths in clear water, but would be pointless in muddy or murky water.

It's really just a matter of using common sense.

As a rule of thumb, I use *lighter line for small-mouths and heavier for largemouths.* For Mr. Big Jaws, the right weight usually falls somewhere between 10- and 20-pound test—strong enough to stand up to the harder hook-set these fishes' tougher

BEST BASS TACKLE

mouths require and to resist breakage in thick cover. The exact weight I choose will depend on the weight and action of the lure. A heavy crankbait or spinnerbait will take 14- or 17-pound test, a topwater lure maybe 10.

If I want my bait to sink quickly, *a lighter line will present less water resistance.* If I want it to run longer near the surface, a heavier line will be better.

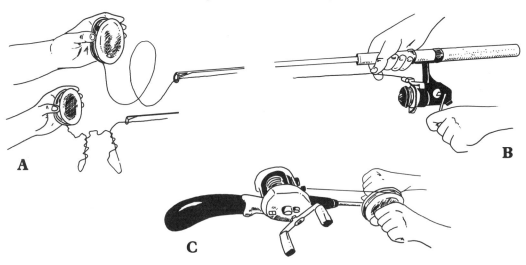

(A) To check for line twist, position rod tip to about one foot from supply spool. If slack line twists, turn supply spool completely around. (B) Keep light tension on line when spooling a spinning reel. (C) To spool a bait-casting reel, you can insert a pencil into the spool to allow the line to move freely. Keep proper tension on the line by asking the person holding the pencil to exert a slight inward pressure on the supply spool.

For smallmouths, I prefer a six to ten-pound test line. Sometimes, if I'm using light jigs I'll go down to a four-pound test. The rule here, based on the visibility factor, is *the clearer the water and slower the presentation, the lighter the line.*

Visibility and lure action also govern the use of such things as sinkers, split shot, split rings, swivels, snaps, swivel-snaps and leaders.

A wire leader is a necessity if you're fishing for

toothy critters such as muskie and northern pike, which can bite right through a piece of monofilament. These fish attack with such slashing speed they probably never see the leader, and even if they do notice it, they're so vicious they probably don't care. Bass, on the other hand, don't bite through lines and—unless they're making an impulse strike against an irritating bait such as a buzzbait—they get mighty suspicious when they see anything that doesn't look natural. I never use a leader on bass, and I also try to keep the use of other bits and pieces of non-natural-looking metal to a minimum. Most crankbaits, for example, come with a split ring already on the lure, so I just tie my line directly onto that. Using anything extra, like a swivel snap, might throw the lure's balance off and affect its action, as well as adding just one more unnatural-looking item. If I use anything on the end of my line, it will usually be just a snap, rather than snap and swivel. About the only thing you'd need a snap and swivel for would be to avoid line twist when using a wobbling spoon. It's the same with shot and sinkers: keep 'em to a minimum.

It's a good idea to check your line frequently for nicks and rough spots, especially after you finish boating a fish that's given you a battle. Run your finger along the first few feet of line and if you feel anything, cut it off and re-tie. I'd rather take the extra time to do that, than stand there cussing because my line broke and I missed a two-pounder. Usually I re-tie every time I boat a fish, as a matter of habit.

Another good habit I've formed has to do with the last bit of terminal tackle—the hook. Keep it sharp. Usually the hooks on a prepackaged lure fresh from the factory aren't sharp enough to do the best job. I automatically sharpen the points on every new lure. The night before a tournament, I go through my rods and tackle box and sharpen every lure I plan to use next day. To check your own hooks, crook your thumb over and slide the tooth of a hook against your thumbnail. If it catches and holds, it's sharp. If it doesn't catch, sharpen it.

ACCESSORIES

Rods, reels and hooks aren't the only things in a tackle shop that can help you catch fish. Whole armies of accessories line the shelves, and their usefulness ranges from marginal to indispensable.

Among the latter items is the landing net. More often than any of us care to recall, that once-in-a-lifetime fish—the tail-walking, head-shaking rod-bender we could already see gracing a plaque on the rec room wall—pops the hook and swims free just when we've got it to the boat. It's no coincidence, but a logical result of the short line and lack of play in the rod at this stage, which make it easier for the fish to lever the hook out of its mouth. In that last yard between lake and livewell, a net can be crucial.

Nets come in a variety of bag sizes, mesh types and handle lengths and are made of various materials. The three basic types are: 1) the stream net, designed for use in shallow water by a fisherman in waders (a 5- or 6-inch handle and a hoop circumference of from 18 to 20 inches); 2) the boat net (a 14-inch to 4-foot handle and an 18- to 24-inch hoop); and, 3) the saltwater or downrigger net (a 5-foot handle and a 24- to 36-inch hoop). For bass, I prefer a boat net with a 4- to 5-foot handle and a hoop circumference of about 24 inches. The net bag should be between 16 and 24 inches deep—24 if you plan on fishing often for largemouths.

The two commonest handle materials are aluminum and wood, and the usual netting material is nylon or cotton. Aluminum is cheaper than wood, but beware of the thin-gauge, hollow-tube aluminum nets sold in corner hardware stores for $5 to $10. Often the gauge on these is so thin that bending or kinking them is nearly impossible to avoid. Although I don't usually throw my nets overboard, some people like the reassurance of having a net that floats. If you buy aluminum, pick a heavier-gauge net (these range in price from $10 for a small stream net to $30 for a boat net). Some brands are also warranted to float. Wooden nets all float, of course, and they are also more durable than their light metal counterparts. They also cost more—from $30 for a small stream net to $100-plus for some of the better boat nets.

If you plan to practise catch-and-release fishing, net material is important. Nylon netting is harder on a fish than cotton, and a coarse weave is more destructive to tissue than a tighter weave. Cotton may deteriorate more quickly than nylon, but the fish will deteriorate more slowly if you scoop it up in a cotton net. So take your choice: a net that lasts a bit longer, or released fish that last longer.

You can also buy nets made with rubber netting. The bag is generally very shallow, and using one is more like using a scoop than a traditional net. Hooks don't tend to get caught as easily in them as they do in other types of net mesh. However, I personally don't like them because the density of the mesh usually offers too much resistance to the water when you try to sweep the net under the surface and up to a fish. It's like paddling with your arms tied. I like to be able to sweep a net quietly and smoothly, without spooking my bass.

Another valuable accessory is a hook sharpener. You can buy a small, Carborundum hand sharpener if you are strictly a weekend angler, or invest in a more costly electric model if you do a lot of fishing. I use an electric sharpener, but of course I sharpen hundreds of hooks each week during the tournament season.

Also useful in locating fish is a surface temperature thermometer. A thermostatic model, such as the type used by photographers to test developing solutions, will do a serviceable job.

ELECTRONIC EQUIPMENT

Serious bassers will eventually want to outfit themselves with some of the electronic aids that have been developed over the past couple of decades, including digital electronic surface temperature gauges, electronic depth-finders, pH meters and color-selector meters. I use all of these tools, and find each of them useful, but be warned in advance—they can be expensive.

Depth-finders come in two basic types, flasher units and graphing units, of which graphs are the more expensive. Flashers use a circular dial and flashing lights to indicate depth and bottom structure, a system that resembles the sonar screen the yeoman on the destroyer in the war movies always looks at to spot the enemy submarine. Chart-type graphs employ a roll of lined graph paper and a needle, which traces the actual contour of the bottom in ink as your boat moves. A still-newer innovation is the liquid crystal recorder (LCR) graph unit. A standard unit costs a trifle less than a graph recorder. Others boast an incredible array of features, including a built-in surface temperature gauge and an eight-color screen that not only tells you where the fish are, but how big they are.

A flasher, priced from $150 to $350, is more than adequate for the average basser. Graphs are generally used by pros, guides, or bassers who fish non-visible deep-water structures such as humps, points and dropoffs. These range in price from $700 to $1,500 for a chart recorder and from $340 to $500 for a liquid crystal unit. A feature-studded, eight-color liquid crystal unit may run as high as $1,700. I prefer liquid crystal units for their many features and ease of use—no paper or stylus to replace.

In choosing a depth-finder, be sure to note its

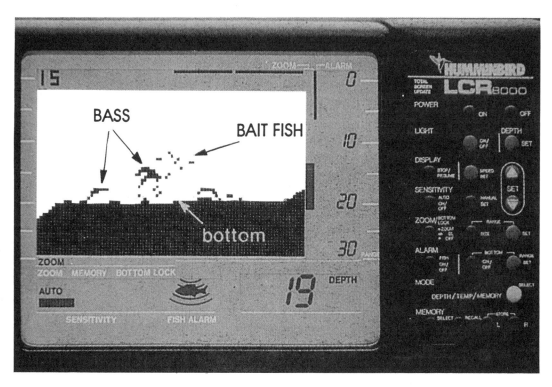

A liquid crystal recorder (LCR) graph unit.

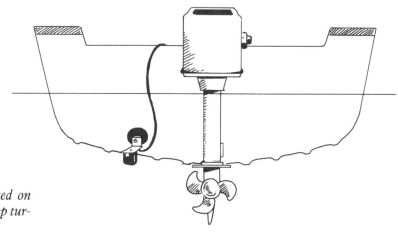

A transducer is mounted on the transom clear of prop turbulence.

depth range and pick one that will correspond to the average depths at which you'll be angling. Just as important is the transducer cone angle of your depth-finder. This is the angle at which the unit's sound waves travel from the boat to the bottom, spreading or fanning out sideways as they move downward. A wide-angle unit will make a wide cone, with its point or apex at the boat and its broad base parallel with the bottom. A narrow-angle unit will produce a narrower cone, whose base on the bottom will occupy a smaller area.

Since most bass fishing is done in relatively shallow water, a wide-angle transducer—from 28 to 32 degrees—will be preferable. The wider the angle, the more bottom area will be "read" at one time as you pass over it. The narrower-angle units—16 or 18 degrees—would cover too small an area on each sweep. They're more practical for deep water fishing, where their sharper focus prevents distorted readings.

An electronic color-selector, which is a kind of advanced version of a photographer's light meter, may well become an indispensable item among pro bassers. It measures water clarity and light refraction and gives a fairly accurate reading of which lure colors will be most visible to fish on a given day in a given body of water. I carry one in my own bass boat and have been experimenting with it for the past few seasons. The results aren't conclusive yet, but they are encouraging. My brother Wayne and I may even have won a tournament because of it.

We had our limit in the livewell when we pulled into a bay with crystal-clear water about three feet deep. The color-selector, which has a rainbow spectrum on it bright enough to pop your eyes out, said "use red." I threw a flipping jig—red with black trim—and nailed two five-pounders on it. Two smaller fish were tossed back, and those big bucks gave us a whopping 32-pound weigh-in total over two days. We took first place.

Of course, whole books could be written on the latest electronic equipment, and the arguments pro and con various features and theories will be raging for years to come. The best bet for someone new to the subject is to spend some time reading the literature—then shop at a tackle merchant you already know you can trust.

Bob holds a color selector; an LCR is mounted on the boat's console to his left.

SOLUNAR TABLES

That about wraps up the tackle a bass fisherman will need, except for one last item: *The Solunar Tables.* I've saved these for last because a lot of fishermen, hunters and scientists claim they're not properly scientific. I've even heard some people call them "superstitious."

Call them what you like. They work. Wayne and I have seen proof of it time and time again. It's almost uncanny. Based on the idea that the movements of the moon and sun in relation to the earth not only affect the tides in the ocean, but also fresh water and the physiology of living things, the tables list major and minor activity or feeding periods for fish and wildlife at various latitudes at various times of the year.

I've been on the water, cruising along in a bass boat on a quiet morning or lazy afternoon, and suddenly marveled as the air, land and water seemed to come alive with birds, fish and foraging animals. I've checked the tables later and found that, sure enough, the activity started just when the tables said a major period was supposed to begin.

Here's a good example. At a bass tournament on Lake St. Clair, a cold front had just passed through and the waves were over five feet high. Fishing was extremely tough. Wayne and I headed into a canal to escape the rough water. As we started working down one bank, we approached a weed bed which was approximately one hundred feet square. Immediately, we each had a fish on. Mine nabbed a crankbait on the edge of the bed and Wayne's a weedless spoon in the middle of the bed. As we continued down the canal, we wondered if there were more fish where we had just been. We both turned around to see the weed bed come alive with surface-feeding largemouth. Some well-placed casts with a Zara-Spook topwater lure produced a quick limit. The fishing lasted about fifteen minutes before they shut off. When we double-checked *The Solunar Tables*, they confirmed that we had hit a major feeding period. During a cold front, the feeding periods of bass will be fast and furious compared to the longer feeding periods during stable weather conditions.

I'm no scientist, and can't argue the case for these tables statistically, but I carry a copy in my boat and another in my van, and consult them before every tournament. A copy costs only about $2 at good tackle shops, and they're worth every penny.

THREE

POPPERS, PLUGS AND PLASTIC WORMS

Sometimes I wonder if lures are designed to catch fish or to catch fishermen. Walk into a good tackle shop and the colors are as wild as a kindergarten kid's crayon box: red, green, yellow, chartreuse, fluorescent pink, motor oil, silver, metal flake—you name it and it's there in every shape and size and with every kind of action. There are rows of spoons, spinners, buzzbaits, crankbaits that look like minnows, crankbaits that look like crayfish, Rattlin Spots, Zara-Spooks, CC Shads, Redfins, Tiny Torpedos, Rednecks—the list goes on. It's enough to make a brand-new basser's brains boil.

Other fishermen don't make it any easier to figure out which ones you need, either. Everybody seems to have their own set of favorites and each one seems to have a *different* set. Tell an old-timer you're going for largemouth, and he'll say get yourself a Hula Popper or a bunch of black plastic worms. A younger guy will tell you to get a buzzbait or spinner. If you don't have a lot of personal experience to go by, you feel as if you're flying blind.

Which lures *are* best for bass, anyway?

The answer, depending on the season and the circumstances in which you find your fish, is almost any lure in the store. I said in Chapter One that, fishing for bass, sooner or later you'll have to use every item in your bag of tricks, and I wasn't exaggerating. With the exception of muskie lures or deep-sea billfish baits, there aren't many lures I

A largemouth caught on a Redneck plastic worm.

haven't caught bass on. There is no single Magic Bass Bait, but a whole range of them designed for a fascinating variety of situations.

ORDER IN CHAOS

Probably the easiest way to see the order behind the chaos is to classify lures by depth (top-water, shallow, mid-depth, deep-diving or bottom baits) and action (whether they're made for fast or slow presentation). Topwater lures, for example, include both fast-presentation buzzbaits that zip across the surface of the water like little motorboats and slow-presentation poppers and floating min-nows, which are designed to lie still on the surface between sudden twitches. Shallow-water lures include both the modern skirted spinnerbaits and the old reliable Mepps spinners, as well as spoons, crankbaits that run just under the surface and plastic worms. Deep-running lures include long-lipped crankbaits designed to dive down as far as ten feet or more, and some spoons, while bottom baits include such slow-presentation standbys as jigs and—fished differently than in shallow-water situations—plastic worms.

Looking at the store shelves with these catego-ries in mind, things start to fall in place. Let's take the groups in descending order.

Bigger, fatter plugs seem to be better suited to largemouth, whose buckets are wide enough to let a house in, while the thinner, pencil-type plugs seem to be better suited to smallmouth.

Topwater lures

There are some researchers who claim that 99 percent of bass strikes on artificial lures are prompted by irritation rather than hunger, by aggressive reflex rather than the feeding instinct. I wouldn't put the percentage quite that high for other lures, but it's certainly true for buzzbaits. A bass has to be pretty angry to chase one of these little beau-ties and nail it. But that Brrrrrrr action seems to do the trick. When they hit a buzzbait, they really bang it.

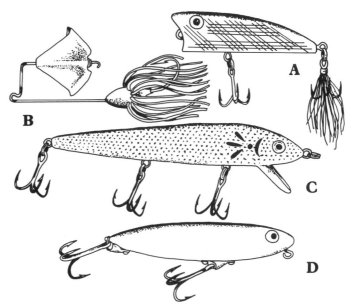

Topwater lures: (A) Pop-R; (B) buzzbait; (C) Redfin; (D) Zara-Spook.

Joe Hughes holds two smallmouths caught on the Pop-R topwater lure.

This largemouth was caught by twitching a Redfin lure across the surface of the water.

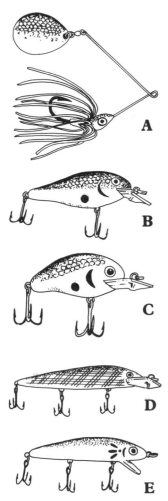

Subsurface lures: (A) safety pin spinnerbait; (B) and (C) shallow-running crankbaits; (D) and (E) floating minnow plugs; (F) weedless spoon.

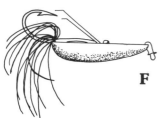

There are two ways to use a buzzer. You can cast it out, let it sink down a few feet, then lift your rod tip up and start reeling it fast, up to the surface where it breaks water, and then across the surface several feet. Then stop and let it flutter down again. I've seen this work for other people, but personally I prefer to cast a buzzbait out, get it up on the surface right away and keep it there. I reel it in at a steady speed, fast enough to keep it planing. I think this lets me cover more water with the lure action working at its optimum than a stop-and-go pattern would. Both methods irritate fish. The stop-and-go pattern first gets their attention, then tempts them to strike what looks like a vulnerable target when the lure stops and flutters down. The steady retrieve just irritates and keeps on irritating until the fish get mad enough to hit. Both patterns work well on largemouths in shallow weed flats.

Other topwater lures call for a slower presentation. Floating minnow baits such as the Rebel or Redfin, and stickbaits or pencil-type plugs require a

This Mister Big Jaws was caught on a weedless spoon.

little patience in the presentation. Cast them out and let them lie on the surface until all of the ripple rings have disappeared. Then jerk or twitch them a foot or two across the water, and let them lie still again. The idea is to get the fish's attention, annoy it enough to make it want to strike, but not make so much of a splash that you spook it. The same method works with poppers. Cast one out and let it lie still until the ripples settle down. Then take an underhand sweep and pop it along about six inches to a foot, and let it lie still again. Both poppers and floating minnows are made to mimic the appearance of live bait—a wounded minnow or frog—but it may actually be curiosity or plain irritation that makes fish hit them.

Subsurface lures

Spinners, spoons and shallow-running crankbaits are more often intended to imitate live bait. The flashing silver of a spinner or oscillation of a spoon suggests the flash of a shiner in the water, while the photo-print finishes of some crankbaits look more like live bait than the live bait itself. Of course no live crayfish or minnow swims along with a bunch of treble hooks sticking out of it and a line attached to its mouth, and if the fish look too closely at a crankbait, they'll notice something isn't right. For that reason, a steady, unbroken retrieve at a speed fast enough to allow the fish a glance, but not a microscopic examination, works best. The actual speed of your retrieve should take water clarity into consideration. If the water is as clear as glass, crank

Remember when you're working a crankbait or spinner that bass aren't the sleek, fast, long-running racers that pike are; don't overdo the speed. There are times when bass will be triggered by a fast-moving lure but varying the speed of the retrieve can be more effective.

the bait in faster. If it's murky or muddy enough to disguise the hooks and line, crank a bit slower and give the fish a chance to home in on the disturbance your bait's action creates in the water. In the latter situation, a rattling lure—a pregnant minnow-type plug with metal bearings inside—is useful.

Some floating minnow plugs with relatively short lips are meant to run at shallow depths and then be twitched down, in a sudden, zipping motion. Cast them out, then twitch the rod tip down sharply to make them dart down about a foot. Let them float up again slowly, then twitch them down again. Fish usually seem to hit as the bait floats up.

As a general rule, when I'm fishing a surface bait I like to keep my rod tip high, around ten or eleven o'clock. With shallow-running lures, I keep it a bit lower, around eight or nine o'clock.

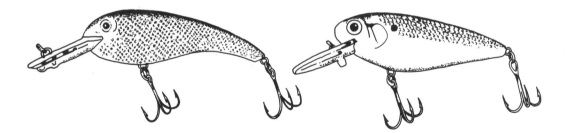

Deep-running crankbaits.

Deep-running lures

Obviously, these do their best work when they're down deep, so the faster you get them down, the better. I usually cast deep-running crankbaits out, dip the tip of my rod down low and crank hard to get them down there. Then I let up a bit and reel them in with a steady retrieve, allowing the action designed into the plug to provide the right motion. After all, with a crankbait, the idea is simply to crank it in.

When I was a kid, fishing Rondeau Bay on the shores of Lake Erie, I had another method that I'd use on both deep-diving and medium-depth plugs. I'd get out on a weed flat where the water was about six feet deep, but the weeds on the bottom only came up about three feet from the mud below. I'd cast out, dip my rod tip and crank that plug down till I felt it hit the weeds. Then I'd stop and let its natural buoyancy float it up clear of the tangle. As soon as it had risen free about two feet, I'd crank it right down again and rip it into those weeds. Most of my hits came when the bait was floating up. I nailed a lot of largemouth that way.

The deep-running crayfish-imitation crankbait is nearly as large as this largemouth fingerling, but the youngster pursued it aggressively.

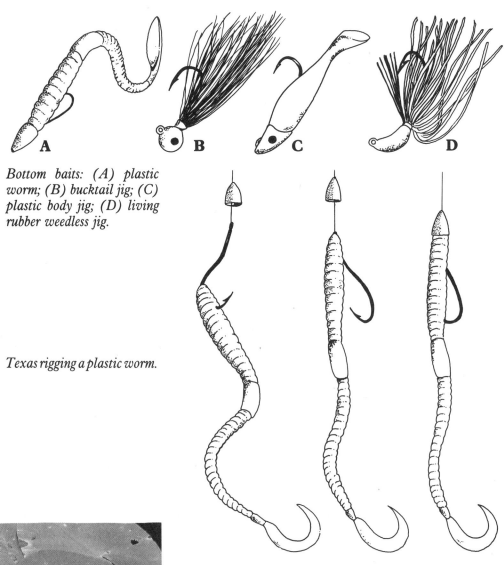

Bottom baits: (A) plastic worm; (B) bucktail jig; (C) plastic body jig; (D) living rubber weedless jig.

Texas rigging a plastic worm.

A Redneck plastic worm rigged Texas-style.

Bottom baits

Plastic worms are a good bait for both deep-water and bottom fishing, and they're one of my favorites. I still remember how much my Dad used to swear by his purple plastic worms. He had a real thing about them to the point where it became a sort of family joke. "Purple worms," he'd say. "Purple worms!" My taste in color is a little different. I tend to prefer black or motor oil, or something with a sparkly metal flake in it, but I like purple worms,

When selecting jigs for bass, use the lightest weight possible for the fishing condition. I've found that a jig that descends slowly is more effective than one that falls like a rock. An ⅛-ounce jig on six-pound line attracts smallmouth on a point and a ⅜-ounce jig on fourteen-pound line works wonders on largemouth in thick weeds.

This jig and pork rind, or "jig and pig," has a weed guard protecting the hook, making it snagless.

too. So do bass, especially when you use the swimming technique. Cast your worm out and let it flutter down until you feel it hit bottom. Then, when the line goes a bit slack and you know it's settled, lift it up. Then let it settle again. (Using a graphite rod helps, because of the sensitive touch it provides.) To swim the worm, pull back and hop it slowly over the bottom for about ten feet and let it settle again. Remember not to jerk it quickly, but to work it slowly. If the bottom cover is thick, use shorter hops when you swim the worm—maybe three to five feet, instead of ten. Bass don't like to travel a long way through the really heavy stuff, down there in the coontail and milfoil, and you want to make it easy for them.

With bottom fishing, the whole key is to watch your line. If you keep your rod tip up at eight or nine o'clock to maintain line tension, you'll frequently see the line move before you feel the nibble. Sometimes you'll see other things moving, too. Once my partner and I were fishing with worms in some pencil reeds, watching for the first sign of a nibble, and we noticed that just before a strike we could sometimes see the weeds move as a swimming fish brushed them aside. Ever since, I've kept my eye not only on my line, but also on everything around it.

Of course, the bottom bait *par excellence* is the jig, and there are so many different jig types, in every weight, color and configuration, you could probably write a book on them alone. It would be worth reading, too. When the fishing gets tough—when the bass are really down deep, or lethargic after the passage of a cold front or the onset of cooler weather in the fall, or the fish just plain aren't reacting to anything you throw them—that little tidbit of a jig does the job.

I've seen it over and over again in tournaments, to the point where I call it "the mint syndrome." Fish are a lot like you and me. If we go out to a

When jig fishing, experiment with your retrieves to find out which one attracts the fish on that particular day. Bass may react differently to the same presentation from one day to the next. Some days they will want a jig worked very slowly on the bottom, other days they will react to a lift-and-drop method and still other days a quick snap of the rod to explode the jig off the bottom will be the answer. The trick is to use different rhythms to find the one that works.

restaurant and put away a huge steak dinner with all the trimmings, and the waitress asks if we want the cheesecake dessert, chances are we'll be too full and say no. But going out the door afterward, we'll pass the cashier's counter and pick an after-dinner mint out of the bowl. A bass is no different. If that old lunker has had a good feed recently, or feels too cold to care about darting after its dinner, towing a fat crankbait past its nose may do nothing for it. Dip a little jig down there under its lip, though, wiggle it around, and that lunker will up and take it. It's an after-dinner mint, and fish always seem to have room for one.

However, they won't have room if you don't present it the right way. You don't just dunk it and jerk it up, dunk it and jerk it up, like a yo-yo. Whether you're using a pork-rind-tipped "jig and pig," a twister or a feathered bucktail, a jig should be worked *slowly*, leisurely, rhythmically, as if both you and the fish had all day. It's a lot like ice-fishing: let the bait down slowly, pull it up steadily but gently, then let it flutter down. The fish will watch it—in clear water you can see them on the bottom, suspended there, eyeing it—until they think, "Oh, why not! It's just a little morsel." Then munch. Most of the time, they seem to take the bait on the downslide, as it flutters or chopper-blades back down after you've pulled it up.

With jigs, as with other slow-presentation lures (especially in clear water), keep foreign-looking attachments to a minimum. Use light line, clear mono- or co-filament, and tie directly onto the jig without any snaps, swivels or what-nots.

Whatever depth you're fishing at and whatever bait you're using, remember to keep your rod tip up. Fishermen seem to have an unconscious tendency (maybe it's anticipation that causes it?) to point their rod tip at the lure as they reel it in. Check yourself sometimes when you're out in the boat.

You'll probably catch yourself doing it.

It's a bad habit, for several reasons. If your rod tip is aimed straight at the lure, all the strain when a fish hits will be on the line itself and the reel, not on the rod. What's the point of having a rod with the power and flexibility to absorb the shock of a fighting fish and the sensitivity to detect the slightest nibble, if you don't use it properly?

COLOR, SCENT AND FISH IMMUNITY

There are many other points to consider when you shop for lures, particularly whether the bait you buy is adapted to the cover you plan to work. If you're going to be fishing in weeds, for example, a weedless lure or one with a safety-pin configuration where the hook points upward may be your best bet. If you're fishing murky or muddy waters, rattling lures, or spinnerbaits with big blades whose actions create a disturbance in the water, will get the attention of bass that are foraging by sound rather than sight.

There are also the factors of color, scent and a problem I refer to as "fish immunity."

Color

As I mentioned in Chapter One, bass appear to be able to detect a wide range of colors and to prefer some over others under certain conditions—especially after mid-season, when they seem to get a bit wiser and more finicky than they were in the spring. It's possible that the new color-selectors may make choosing your hues automatic if they prove to be consistently accurate over time. Some lure manufacturers are already banking on them and are marketing packages of several like-colored lures, color-coded to match the spectrum on a color-selector dial. If the selector says Wild Man Red is the color for the day, you can whip out a package of five different baits—all of them Wild Man Red, or neon yellow, or whatever. There are tackle boxes on the market with compartments organized to file lures by color, and stores sell waterproof-paint kits so that you can give your old baits a face-lift to match the colors on the selector dial.

If you don't own a selector, you'll have to go by the time-honored system followed by anglers since fishing began: trial and error. I have personal favorites. For example, in the early season, fishing for smallmouths, I've really slaughtered them on ⅜-ounce white spinnerbaits. Not green or chartreuse, but white. In the springtime, they just seem to love that color. I also like motor oil plastic worms, and in dark water I use chrome tones and fluorescent colors—fluorescent red or chartreuse.

There is also an old rule of thumb: dark days, dark lures; bright days, bright lures. But I think the only rational rule I've heard is "give 'em what they're eating." If you're fishing the Great Lakes in an area where the bass are hitting emerald shiners, give them chrome. If you're fishing rocks for smallmouths and know there are a lot of crayfish around, give them brownish, crayfish-colored lures. Of course they may hit other colors, too. You have to experiment and get a feel for what they seem to like in your favorite spots at various times of the year. The basic message is, color *is* important. If they aren't grabbing at one color, try another and you may hit the jackpot.

Bass in clear water use their sense of sight more than bass in murky water do. However, the latter have a much better sense of hearing. Noisy, bright lures attract dirty water bass and more subtle natural lures attract clear water fish.

Scent

Bait manufacturers have capitalized on the upsurge in angler interest in scent by turning out a whole battery of smelly baits. The names sound like something a perfume salesman would come up with if he went nuts—Essence of Nightcrawler, Walleye Elixir, Essence of Cricket—but the idea behind them is logical, and I've seen proof that they can work.

One example was a tournament I fished a couple of years back. My partner and I were working a river leading to a lock, flipping for largemouth along the banks. If we ever wanted an acid test of a lure's worth, this was it. The traffic in that river was something else—large boats roared by every five minutes, their wakes stirring up the water and sending waves sloshing against the banks. The water had already been worked by just about everybody in the tournament, and by rights there shouldn't have been any fish left to catch. On top of everything else, my partner had the bow position and got first crack at every spot we tried. We were both using the same methods and same baits, with one exception: I'd coated my bait with scent, and my partner hadn't.

The results were hard to argue with. I took four largemouths, all over two pounds, and my partner caught zip. It was enough to convince me that scent baits work, at least in some situations.

Unfortunately, our knowledge of the way fish use their sniffers is still pretty sketchy. For example, nobody yet knows whether using the pheromones given off by fish during spawning would attract bass or turn them off. Because feeding activity decreases during spawning, it's possible that smelling this scent would take away a lunker's appetite. But fish, especially males, are very aggressive during spawning and will strike at anything that looks as if it's invading their territory. Maybe the mating pheromones would trigger fish into striking.

Of course, a real sportsman doesn't go after spawning fish on their beds anyway, but the illustration shows the kind of gaps there are in what we know. I don't have all the answers, and neither does anybody else at this stage of the game. Personally, I carry several plastic squeeze bottles of scent bait in my tackle box and use them regularly. If I have to make engine repairs on the water, every lure I touch afterward gets a shot of scent. If I catch a pike, that lure gets sprayed with scent before I use it again. In fact, I often just squirt a jet of scent on each lure I use, regardless of the situation. Over the long haul, I think it boosts the odds in my favor.

My experience so far seems to indicate that scent baits work best in slow-presentation situations and cooler temperatures, such as jigging for small-mouths after a cold front has passed through. This makes a certain amount of sense. After all, if a fish hits a flashing spinnerbait as it zips by, it's more likely a result of visual reflex than of the fish's sense of smell. It's also possible that because fish are less active in cold weather, they may need the added stimulus of scent to provoke them into striking. It could be that coating a plastic worm with scent bait also gives it more of the slimy feel fish seem to like.

Whatever the real reasons are, I'm sure they make sense to the fish, and your best bet is to try to let them tell you what to do. If you find they go wild for *parfum de nightcrawler* at dawn on your favorite pond, then give them parfum de nightcrawler.

Of course, the longer a scent bait clings to a lure, the greater the chance of getting good results. Several lure-makers produce baits with fuzzy coatings that absorb and hold scent baits longer than plain plastic or wood. I find this particularly helpful with jigs, and keep a good supply of fuzzy ones in my tackle box.

One note of warning on scent baits, however: they're chemicals, and so are the plastic materials your lures are made of. When you're through fishing for the day, don't leave a bunch of scent-coated plastic worms lying unwashed in your tackle box. The next time you look in the tray, those worms may be a mass of useless goo. Rinse them off first, then store them in the box. The same is true of the lures themselves. Some brands of plastic worm may react with the plastic in certain crankbaits, sticking to them or melting them. Make sure they don't touch one another when you put them away.

Fish immunity

As for the problem I referred to earlier as "fish immunity," I'm convinced it's a real factor. Fish seem to be no different than other living things when they get hurt: they learn from their hard knocks and grow wary with age. Some lures are traditional standbys. They've been hauling in lunkers for years and have wondrous reputations based on their past performances. But I believe, over time, fish become suspicious of them—maybe even bored by them—and eventually they lose some of their power of attraction. Back in the heyday of Rondeau Bay, certain lures produced more fish than others. One was the black Bayou Boogie. It was the hot bait on the bay for a few years until the fish caught on. Then the tackle store couldn't give them away.

I try new lures constantly, and my tackle box tends to be a reflection of the current state of the art, rather than a course in angling history. Don't get me wrong. I'm not saying those old-timers don't still catch fish. They do. I'm just saying that I have a personal bias toward staying at the cutting edge of the newest ideas in my field. I suppose I'm a little like a gambler, always on the lookout for a foolproof system to beat the odds, or an entrepreneur looking for the greatest business in the world. I'm always hoping to find the greatest bass bait in the world, and I don't think I'll ever become complacent enough to quit searching for it.

Maybe the newest fluorescent color, or noisemaker, or buzzbait action will give me the edge in the next tournament. Can I afford to pass it up? Can you?

There are a lot worse things to spend our money on than the possibility of catching more bass.

FOUR

LETHAL LIVE BAITS

I highly recommend a chemical called Catch and Release for anglers who intend to release their catch. This chemical will help insure a better live release for bass that may have been mishandled. A tablespoon of these crystals in your livewell will sedate the fish and replace any protective slime that may have been removed from the fish while handling it. There is a higher risk of a fungus developing on the fish if this chemical is not used.

Stomach contents of a bass— two rock bass and a cray- fish—that were found in a livewell after the fish was weighed in and released at a tournament.

There's no question about it: live baits are lethal. In fact, that's a major reason why a lot of catch-and-release anglers don't use them and why most tournament rules exclude them. Even a hungry bass, once it notices the strange feel of a balsa crankbait or plastic worm in its mouth, is unlikely to swallow it. But give that same fish a real worm or a squirming frog or crayfish, and "gloop," it's down the hatch.

With an artificial lure, when you set the hook the barb usually catches on the fish's bony jaw where it does very little damage. With live bait, if you give the fish too much time before you set the hook, it's already been swallowed. If this happens, you should cut the line and leave the hook inside, where the fish's stomach acids may dissolve it, rather than try removing the hook.

THE NATURAL LOOK

The key to success with live-bait fishing is to make sure that what you put in front of the fish both looks and acts natural.

Unlike artificials, which trigger as many im- pulse strikes based on aggression and territoriality as on anything else, live baits are meant primarily to spark the feeding urge—and every gourmet chef knows that looks can make the meal. Snaps, swivels, heavy line, leaders, over-sized hooks—anything unnatural will turn fish off. Clear, light line, small hooks and minimum use of sinkers and other such gear will have the opposite effect.

When I fish for smallmouth with live bait in open water, I use a number six or eight hook, clear, six- to ten-pound test line, and I tie my line directly onto the hook, without snaps or leaders. Spinning tackle seems to work best with these light lines, and I prefer a longer, five-foot-nine-inch to six-foot medium-action rod.

The reason I use a medium-action rod is that a stubby pool cue would overpower the rest of the rig. If you tried to set the hook with it, not only could your six-pound test line break like a piece of thread, but the tiny wire hook itself could snap in two. Even if it didn't break, because of its size, it could pull right out of the fish's mouth. With a medium-action rod, on the other hand, you just sort of sweep the line in. There's plenty of give.

Of course, these are just my personal preferences. Some live-bait anglers like an old-fashioned bamboo pole, and I have friends who work crayfish with a fly rod/spinning reel combination (it works, I've seen it!).

Every fisherman seems to have his own pet tackle combinations, but one thing they seem to agree on is the best method of live-bait presentation. It's spelled: S.L.O.W. With artificial lures, letting the fish look too closely can be risky. But with natural baits, the closer they look the better, because they're looking at the real thing. You're tempting their taste buds, and patience is the key.

Even when I feel a hit, I still take it slow, giving the fish plenty of time to swallow the bait before I set the hook. I've watched fish in an aquarium swim around with a nightcrawler hanging half-in, half-out of their mouths for quite a while before they gulp it all down. If the part still dangling from your fish's chops is the one with the hook in it, and you pull up too soon on your rod, all you'll get is the hook and a maimed worm. I usually give a bass at least a ten-count before setting the hook, sometimes more.

Here's how I play some of the best bass live baits.

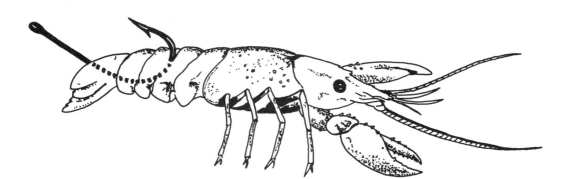

Hook crayfish through the tail, barb up.

Crayfish

As already mentioned, this is the favorite food of smallmouths, but largemouths like crawdads too and will feed on them when they're available. The best kind of crayfish to use are those that have just recently molted and are consequently soft-bodied. Bass seem to look on these as gourmet fare, while the hard-shell variety is merely everyday stuff. Some fishermen go to the extra trouble of removing the crayfish's claws before using them as bait, on the theory that this makes them still more attractive as a dinner. Personally, I've never noticed any difference in the attracting power of clawless crawdads, and don't bother doing it.

LETHAL LIVE BAITS

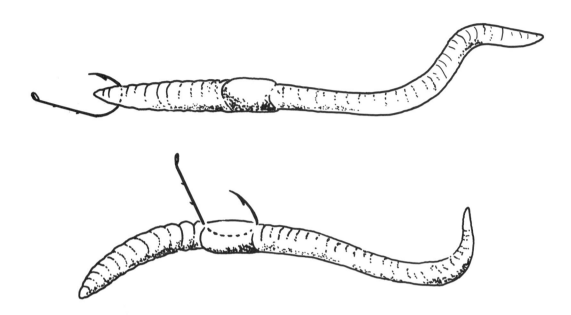

Two ways to place a hook in a night crawler.

Crayfish, of course, swim backward, jetting along tail-first in a burst of speed when they spot an enemy coming, so the right way to put them on your line is to hook them through the tail, barb up. That way, when you reel in they'll move backward. (Some anglers, to keep their bait lively for a longer time, avoid penetrating even the tail and tie the hook to the crayfish with a piece of thread or an elastic band. This is a little too perfectionist for me, though.) In calm water, crayfish are usually heavy enough to sink without the aid of extra weight or sinkers on the line, although sometimes in current I'll put a split shot or two on the line about a foot or so up from the hook where it won't be noticeable. Cast them out, then let the crayfish alone for a while before you reel in.

Some fishermen just let them alone, period, allowing them to crawl along the bottom at their own speed until a fish spots them and makes a move. That works, but I like to cover water more quickly and so I reel my bait in. Usually, I reel very slowly, just barely turning the crank handle, and every now and then give a little pull to make the crayfish hop, as if it were jetting away from danger. This makes it conspicuous.

Worms

The oldest, most popular fish bait in the world is probably the angleworm, and it's to be expected that a fat nightcrawler will work wonders on bass, especially largemouth in shallow-water situations. There are many ways to put a nightcrawler on a hook. Kids fishing for panfish usually thread them on lengthwise, impaling the worm from end to end. Of course, this cuts down the amount of worm that can get nibbled away from the hook by a sunfish without actually taking the hook in its mouth—which is probably why kids do it that way. But it kills the worm quickly, and its squirmy action along with it.

If you're fishing for bass, the more squirmy action you can get out of that nightcrawler the better. Either hook the worm through the nose only, letting its long body dangle free, or rig it Texas-style. In a Texas rig, the hook point is inserted through the worm's nose-end, turned and pushed back out, then brought down to the worm's "belt" and inserted again, leaving the barb inside the worm where fish can't spot it (see page 60). As this puts only two holes in the worm, it will live longer than if it had been threaded on lengthwise, but not as long as when hooked through the nose only.

After the worm is on the hook, cast it out and then drag it in slowly, or hop it or swim it a little bit at a time along the bottom. Flipping works well with nightcrawlers, as it does with plastic worms, and the attractiveness of a jig can triple if you tip it with a worm. I use a jig and worm sometimes fishing for largemouth on weed flats where the weeds are thick. I look for openings in the weeds where the bass like to lie and just dunk the jig right down there.

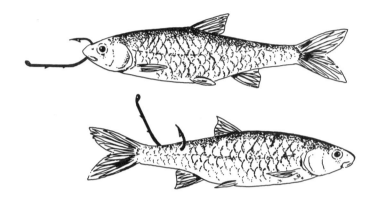

Hook a minnow through the jaws or through the back when fishing it with a bobber.

Minnows

One of the secrets of using live bait effectively is to match your bait to the forage available to fish in the area you're covering. If you're fishing for smallmouth on a rock pile full of crayfish, obviously crayfish are the bait to use. And if you're fishing on the Great Lakes where minnows are the main forage, a minnow is what you need.

On the Great Lakes, the most popular minnow is probably the lake shiner or emerald shiner. A lot of the guys who drift for smallmouth or troll for them use the shiner. The most popular size seems to be three to four inches. Also popular is the creek chub. This species tends to be a little larger than the shiner, four to five inches, as well as more durable. Chubs seem to remain active longer on the hook. If I'm using live bait, I prefer the chub. They seem to be almost a delicacy to bass.

Unlike a long worm, which takes a bit of time for a fish to suck in, a very small minnow can be gulped down in a flash. Schooling fish are competitive, however, and you can get a whole school's appetite up by the simple trick of fishing with a larger chub. When one fish takes it, the chub's tail will hang out of its mouth for a while before it is swallowed, and the other fish in the school will chase the first one, trying to snatch the chub away. After you've pulled the first fish in, the rest of the school will be primed to strike when you cast again.

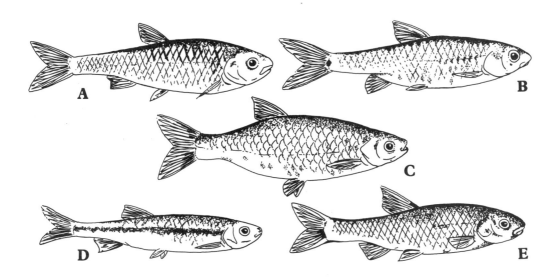

Minnows: (A) common shiner; (B) spottail shiner; (C) golden shiner; (D) emerald shiner; (E) chub.

(Down in the southern United States, they have another trick. They'll tie on a small bullhead and cast it out over a bass bed. The bullhead will dive right down for the bed, after the eggs, and the bass will hit it hard. This strikes me as sort of dirty pool, though, to deliberately go after spawning fish.)

The best way to hook minnows is through the upper jaw and nostril, or through both jaws, with the barb facing up. Many live-bait users hook them through the back, but all this does is kill them quickly and leave a limp, rather than active, bait on your hook. The only time I hook a minnow through the back is when I'm fishing it with a bobber.

Frogs

Actually, I don't like to fish with frogs. Maybe it's a hangover reaction from watching them being dissected in high school biology class, but I don't like to put the hook into them. Of course that's a personal quirk, and I have to admit frogs are a good bait, especially in lily pads and shallow areas where they are a regular part of the largemouth's diet.

The way to hook them is through the nose or the fleshy part of one hind leg. This minimizes the injury and keeps them lively longer. The way to play them is, again, slowly. Cast them out and leave them alone for a time before you move them along the bottom. They'll swim around themselves and attract attention.

Other live baits

There are many other live baits that work on bass. Grasshoppers and crickets are probably the best insect baits, and, as with crayfish, some fishermen tie the hook to the bug with a piece of thread to avoid injuring it and to keep it lively longer. Waterdogs, the aquatic stage of the tiger salamander, are also a good bass bait.

Leeches are good warm-water baits, too, with an irresistible wriggling/undulating action. But I don't think even a perfectionist would try to tie a hook to one of these little devils! Obviously, the best way to use them is to hook them through the head, like a worm.

A RULE OF THUMB

Besides matching the bait to the forage available in a particular area, there is another rule of thumb in live-bait fishing: the colder the water, the slower the bait. If a cold front has passed by and the water is chilled right down, the fish are going to be lethargic. They won't have the energy to go dashing after a fast buzzbait or even a crankbait that darts by them too quickly. Swim a little green worm slowly past them, though, or tempt them with a persistent jig and they'll get up the energy to hit.

It's common sense, after all.

FIVE

THROWING A LURE, PLAYING A FISH

Once you've chosen balanced tackle and bought the baits you know will drive bass nuts, you still have to find fish, put your lure in front of them and, when that big boy hits, get him into your landing net. Accurate casting and a good grasp of the basics of playing a fish are essential. (We'll cover the fine points of fish locating in the next chapter.)

FLING THAT THING

Fishing has its own set of Murphy's Laws, two of which seem to afflict the apprentice caster more than anyone else: 1) first casts are never long enough, and, 2) lures are aerodynamically constructed so as to land anywhere except on target. Ask the greenest angler on the lake and he'll swear it's true. You can spot him by the glassy look in his eye as his casts fall consistently short of the spot where a lunker is lurking, or overshoot it by a foot, wrapping his line around an overhanging willow branch.

The way to avoid such frustration, whether you're a beginner or an old-timer who's gotten a little rusty, is first to review the basics, then practise.

And practise.

Remember, it doesn't take muscle to throw a bait. If the lure and plug you're using to practise with are the right weight (a ¼-ounce practice plug and six-pound test line for a medium-action spinning rod and a ⅝-ounce plug and ten-pound test line

Fighting a fish with a spinning rod and reel. Be sure to keep the tip up letting it bend rather than pointing it at the fish.

for a bait-casting rig), the rod will do all the work for you. That, after all, is one of the main reasons why the manufacturers went to all the trouble to build so much strength and spring into it. All you have to supply are a limber wrist, good sense of timing and smooth, relaxed movement.

Before starting, make sure there's enough line on your reel to flow easily and not drag against the spool edge as it peels off. Fill an open-faced spinning reel to at least an eighth of an inch from the top edge of the spool. A bait-casting reel should be filled to the point where the spool begins to flare out.

With the right amount of line and a heavy enough plug, you're ready to start practising. Put a hula hoop or an old inner tube or some other target on the ground and move back about fifteen yards or so. Let a bit of line out, enough to allow the plug to dangle four or five inches from the rod tip, and sight in on your target. You should stand at a slight angle to the target, with your elbow bent and just a bit out from your body, and your rod-hand and foot slightly forward. Your rod tip should be at about the ten o'clock position, so that, in your line-of-sight, it makes a vertical line through the spot you want to hit.

If you're using a spinning rod, your hand should grip the rod handle with the thumb on top and fingers underneath the rod, index finger lightly holding the line. The reel and line guides of the rod should both be underneath the rod, as they would be when retrieving a lure, and the bail should be open.

If you're using a bait-casting rig, hold the grip like you would a pistol, but with the reel facing to one side, rather than straight up (to the left if you cast with your right hand, to the right if you're a southpaw). Your thumb should rest lightly on the spool, just touching the line. In this position the line guides will also face to the side, which means you'll be casting against the natural "set" of the rod blank.

The correct hand position on a spinning outfit. Your index finger should cradle the line to give added sensitivity when working a slow-moving bait.

In casting competitions, where accuracy is the only goal and no fish are likely to hit the practice plug, some casters will loosen the blank and rotate it in its seat so that the line guides are facing upward. This gives a bit more power and smoothness. On the water, however, it wouldn't be practical to try this. While you're fooling around with the blank, a lunker could hit you and take everything away in a rush—line, lure and loosened rod blank. In bait-casting, after a cast is made, the angler usually switches hands for the retrieve, holding the grip in the left hand (if he casts right) and cranking with his right. In this position the reel and line guides are upright and the rod's natural set will be able to come into play against a fish if it bites.

The basic movement in casting is the same, regardless of whether you're using a spinning or bait-casting rod. It consists of three parts, usually described as "dip, back and out," but it is one movement. (Remember St. Patrick with his famous example of the three-leafed clover—still one plant?) Thinking of it as three parts helps to describe it, but in action the flow must be continuous and unbroken.

The initial dip of the rod tip "loads" the rod, giving it its power. The greater the initial dip, the

Casting technique: (A) initial dip "loads" the rod; (B) using the wrist only, bring rod tip up and back; (C) still using wrist only, bring rod forward again and out.

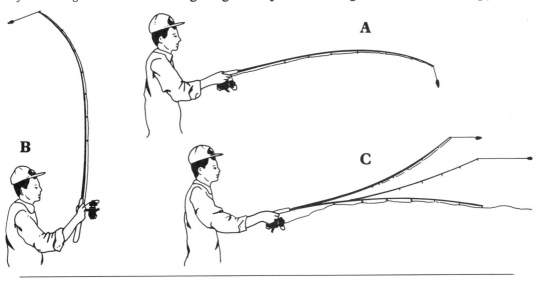

harder the rod will be able to throw the lure. Simply drop the tip down, letting the lure's weight and gravity bend it.

Then, using only your wrist, not your arm, bring the rod tip up and back so that it bends in the opposite direction behind your head, with the plug sailing backward.

Finally, still using your wrist, bring the rod forward again and out, releasing your index finger from the line (if you're spinning) or easing thumb-pressure on the spool (if you're bait-casting) to allow the lure to sail forward freely. The point of release, and the amount of dip you put into the rod tip when you started, will determine the length of your cast. If you release the line too late, the angle of flight will be too low to give you any distance. Release too soon and the lure will make a high, lobbing arc, like a pop-fly in baseball, or even fall behind you.

Bait-casters have to be particularly careful in judging how much to ease off thumb pressure on the spool during a cast. Too much pressure will shorten the lure's flight or stop it in midair. Too little will let the spool turn too fast, giving you one of those rat's nest "professional overruns" mentioned in Chapter Two. Practice will show you at what point to release the line to place your lure at various distances.

Left-right or side-to-side accuracy works a little like swinging a driver in golf: you have to avoid "hooking." Ideally, when a cast is completed, your rod tip should be in the same position it was in when the cast began, bisecting the target and at the same angle to the ground. If you kept your back straight and didn't allow the vertical arc of your cast to deviate from straight up-and-down, the lure should land on target. If it doesn't, it means you've put a hook into the back portion of the cast. If the lure lands to the left of the target, you're round-housing from too far to the right on your back/out stroke. If it lands to the right, you're round-housing from too far to the left.

Another common cause of backlashes among beginning bait-casters is the unconscious tendency to straighten out the elbow at mid-cast to "help" the lure along. Your elbow should stay bent through the dip, back and most of the out phase of the casting motion, not straightening until the tip of the descending rod has passed it and the released lure is in flight. If you straighten it before that, you'll break the cast and pay for it with an immediate bird's nest.

Looking at stop-motion films and analyzing each part of a cast—the way Olympic athletes analyze each aspect of a high-dive or hurdle jump— would reveal still more details of casting form. But I don't think the average fisherman needs to know that much about it, or to think about it that much. Essentially, you should practise the basic motion until it feels right and you find yourself hitting the mark. Then just do it that way—so it "feels" right— on the water. Remember when you were a kid learning to ride your two-wheeler bike, and you looked back and realized the person running along behind you wasn't holding onto the fender anymore? It's the same thing. Learn it, then forget about it.

When fishing boat docks and overhanging willow trees, side-arm casting with a bait-casting outfit or pitching with a spinning rod and reel can be very effective. A five-and-a-half-foot bait-casting rod is easy to use for an underhanded, low-trajectory cast. The key is to get the lure up and under the cover that you are fishing. Pitching with a spinning rod and reel is another method for getting into these hard-to-reach places. By dropping a rod's length of line off your reel and using a pendulum-type motion with your bait, you can place the lure just about anywhere. For exact placement, it is important to feather the spool with your index finger as it is approaching the target. Neither method will spook shallow-water fish because of the low angle the lure travels before it touches down. Some backyard practice will help you master both of these techniques.

Flipping allows you to place a lure in a small place with little or no splash.

FLIPPING—A VERY SPECIAL TECHNIQUE

No discussion of bass fishing techniques would be complete without a word on the very special art of flipping. My favorite combination of rod and reel for this kind of work is a seven-and-a-half-foot, heavy-action rod, with 17- to 25-pound test line and a reel built specifically for the purpose.

The technique itself was inspired by the old-time cane pole methods, particularly one called "tule dipping," which U.S. bass pro Dee Thomas adapted for use in tournament conditions with a bait-casting rod. You don't cast with a cane pole, of course. You just swing the bait out pendulum-style and let it plop straight down in the spot where you want it. Flipping is a sort of combination of this pendulum swing and the hand line-stripping technique used by fly fishermen.

Assuming you're using a seven-and-a-half-foot rod, the sequence goes as follows. First, with your left hand, strip or pull off enough line from the reel to make a 20-foot flip. This means that, with your rod pointing straight up and your left hand extended out to the side holding the stripped-off line, the bait should be dangling about even with the rod butt (see page 85). Next, holding the line loosely between your left thumb and fingers, let the rod tip fall below the level of the butt and, using your right wrist, swing the rod forward with an underhand motion so that the bait starts to move like a pendulum. After gauging where you want the lure to hit, flip the bait forward and guide it to a soft landing, using the restraining pressure of your left hand to control the distance traveled. It takes a little practice and some getting used to, but once you've mastered the technique, you'll be able to place a lure in a very small area almost soundlessly, with little or no splash.

That's the idea in flipping: silence, no muss no fuss. It's a shallow-water technique, and comes in handiest when you want to avoid spooking a big fish in tight quarters. Using it, you can drop your bait almost vertically down into weed pockets, or between the tangled branches of a fallen-over tree, right where Mister Big Jaws is waiting. You can flip many kinds of baits, but the most popular ones are probably living rubber jigs, plastic worms, such as the Redneck or Gator Tail, and pork rinds, along with an assortment of flexible plastic frogs, lizards or insects.

Try it, bass like it.

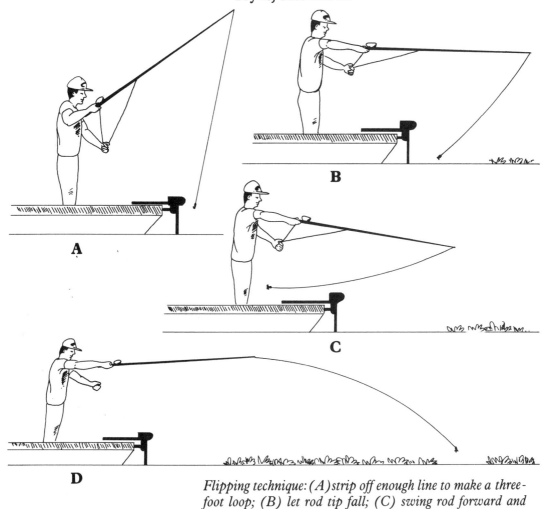

Flipping technique: (A) strip off enough line to make a three-foot loop; (B) let rod tip fall; (C) swing rod forward and start bait moving like a pendulum; (D) flip bait forward.

NEGOTIATING FISH

The art of playing a hard-fighting fish to the net, like many arts, is based partly on logic and the laws of physics and partly on sheer talent. There's no doubt about it, some fishermen and women are better at it than others. But anyone can learn enough about it to fill a livewell if they keep a few rules in mind, and the most important rule is: don't force and horse, "negotiate" your fish.

Step one in most man-versus-fish confrontations is setting the hook, and to do it right the hook has to be sharp. Whenever you buy a new bait, remember to sharpen the hooks, and keep an inexpensive sharpener in your tackle box to touch lures up from time to time. As for the set itself, when you feel a fish strike and are sure it has the bait in its mouth, give a good, sharp snap straight up—not to the side.

For a good hook-set, snap your rod straight upward using your forearms and wrist.

With few exceptions (I'll talk about them shortly), an upright hook-set is crucial. You can miss as many as 50 percent of your strikes by trying to set the hook sideways or down—maybe more than 50 percent with bass. The reasons are simple. First, the bony bottom jaw where a fish's teeth are located is harder for a hook to penetrate than is the fleshier upper jaw, and it's also hinged, which means it can flex and give way from the hook's pressure. The upper jaw, being in rigid line with the fish's whole body, can't spring away from your set as easily. Also, many lures, such as the typical spinnerbait, have hooks that face point-upward, so an upward set is more likely to put them where you want them.

Once you've set the hook, don't let your line go slack, even for an instant. Keep the rod tip up and the pressure on. A big bass can spit your bait with surprising ease if you let the tension break.

Acrobats that like to jump can be especially difficult. When a bass goes airborne there is a natural tendency—a sort of angler's buck fever—to pull back on the line and jerk the fish toward you through the air. Resist that urge, or you'll lose the fish. Yanking a flyer through the air will bring it toward the boat faster than your cranking hand can reel in line, and when it hits the water again your line will suddenly go slack. Ptui! It will spit your lure and be on its way laughing. The right way to react when a bass takes off is to reel—not pull—it in.

As already noted, there are some situations where an upright hook-set isn't called for, despite its general advantages. It doesn't make sense, for example, to try to make an upright set when you're using crankbaits with treble hooks that hang down from the lure's underside. Snapping the rod upward with one of these will bump the top of the lure—where there aren't any hooks—against the fish's upper jaw, failing to hook him and making him flinch away, instead. In such cases, it's better to either set the

◀◀ Plenty of anglers stiffen up when they get their first glance at a big bass on the line. Then they lose it. Your arms and body should act as an extension of your rod while playing a fish. As the bass goes for a power dive, bend with it. By doing this, you absorb some of the stress put on your rod, reel and line. It's amazing how many more fish can be landed by using your body in the fight.

hook down, or not set it at all: just start reeling and keep reeling to maintain line pressure.

This technique works better with the new cofilament line than with monofilament. Monofilament stretches when tension is applied to it, and direct-reeling without a prior hook-set could produce that brief moment of slack during which a fish can spit your lure. Cofilament line doesn't stretch, and direct-reeling can thus keep the pressure on without dangerous interruptions. I've been catching a lot of bass this way lately, especially smallmouth. I find that keeping the rod tip down and reeling hard also tends to minimize jumping, resulting in better control of my fish.

Two other key factors in battling bass are setting your reel drag correctly and heading off runs.

The drag is what wears down an energetic fish and makes it weak enough to bring to your net without snapping the line. It produces sufficient pressure to tire a bass, but lets up before the tension on the line passes the test limit. I like to set my drag fairly tightly, almost up to the test strength of the line I'm using. I count on being able to back-reel fast enough if the fish decides to run. But not everybody is experienced enough to do this. It's probably wiser for most anglers to set their drag more lightly.

A good setting for a beginning-to-intermediate fisherman might be around one-quarter to one-half the line test strength. That way, there's some give if a major-league bass smacks you. You can tighten up the drag control afterward, when the fight is underway and the danger of a hard strike snapping the line has passed. The drag will also help you control runners, shortening the length of their runs.

It's hard to predict when a fish will blast off, but where bass are concerned most runs aren't very long. Beginning anglers are sometimes afraid a fish will run so far that their line will play out and snap. But it's almost unheard-of for a bass to spool you.

It's more likely for a running bass to duck into nearby weeds or brush and snag your line, than to run straight out and pop free.

Whether a run is short or long, however, the fisherman's job is to control it, turn it to his advantage and bring that long-distance lunker back home. The best way to do that is to keep your rod tip up and keep the pressure on. If the drag's tight enough, only a true bruiser will be able to power-run hard

The best way to land a bass if you don't have a net is by grasping its lower lip and hoisting it into the boat.

enough to put you in trouble. It helps, if you sense that your quarry may be the type that likes to travel, to move your boat out toward open water, away from any weeds or deadfalls near shore.

In the rare instance where you get a real track

star on the hook and its run is taking it dangerously near some line-tangling obstacle, the ultimate solution may be to just put the brakes on hard—with thumb pressure or the crank handle—and trust that your line will hold. Nine times out of ten it will hold, and you'll turn the fish.

Place the net in the water and let the person who is fighting the fish lead it into the mesh.

The last leg of every fish's trip to your livewell is the point where it's ready to net, and it's important to remember that you can lose it as easily here as at any point in the preceding tussle.

When a fish is close to your boat, there isn't as much stretch or elasticity in the line as there was when there were several yards of it on the water. With cofilament, there's virtually no give at all. It's possible at this juncture for a spooked fish to make a sudden flip, or start a panicked run, and snap the line or spit the lure. For this reason, it's a good idea, first, not to spook the fish and, second, to try to net it as soon as it's within range of your fishing partner's or your outstretched net-arm. Whoever handles the net should already have it in the water as the fish comes to the boat, rather than suddenly slapping it in just as your big, exhausted bass swims alongside. Slip the net in quietly and hold it waiting underwater as you guide the fish into it.

As an added precaution when boating a bass with a spinning rod, I leave the reel bail open with my index finger against the spool. That way, if the fish takes off, I can release my finger and let line out fast, then feather the line again with my finger to slow down the fish. With a bait-casting rod, I keep my thumb on the free-spool button and hit it if the bass starts to run, then use thumb pressure on the spool to control the race.

There are, of course, many other factors involved in fighting fish, depending on the individual situation, the tackle you're using and even the fish's personality. A good grasp of the above fundamentals, however, will make you a consistent winner on the water. They may sound simple at first, but as any good athlete will tell you, it can take a lifetime to learn to do a simple thing well.

SIX	# FINDING FISH, FISHING SMART

Fishing is a little like the old African recipe for elephant stew, that starts: "First, find an elephant...." The best tackle in the world and the most eye-popping lures money can buy won't amount to a hill of horse apples if you're not "on fish," and finding bass can be a tough proposition.

"Ninety percent of the fish are in ten percent of the water," the saying goes, and looking for them is as much a matter of eliminating the badlands where they aren't, as of finding the hotspots where they are. Knowing their general life cycles and daily activity patterns is basic to both processes, as is good advance scouting, or reconnaissance, of the area you plan to fish. The search for bass, in fact, is an artful science, part logic and part instinct, and it should begin long before you're on the water.

MOVE WITH THE BEAT

As the general descriptions of bass in Chapter One indicated, life underwater follows definite rules—sometimes complicated and hard-to-predict rules—but rules nevertheless. Clue into the main ones, and you'll begin to understand why fish are in one spot one day, and somewhere else the next. You can never figure it all out, of course. I've been working at it most of my life and just scratched the surface. But the more you study fish, the clearer the picture gets, and the heavier your stringer will get, too.

A largemouth caught by flipping under willow trees overhanging a river.

Fish activities over a year are a bit like the parts to a piece of music. The big, seasonal movements from deep water to shallow water and back are like a basic tune, the daily routine shifts are like a steady beat in the background, and the individual coincidences and adventures that happen to each fish are like solos—all different. The way to become fish smart is to listen to the tune and move with the beat.

Start with the seasons. In the winter, of course, bass are fairly inactive, suspended in deep water, and it takes some time after spring breakup before they lose that winter lethargy and begin to move again. When they do, it's to spawn. There's a general move from deep to shallow water, where largemouth and smallmouth make their beds and lay their eggs.

Location of bass during the winter.

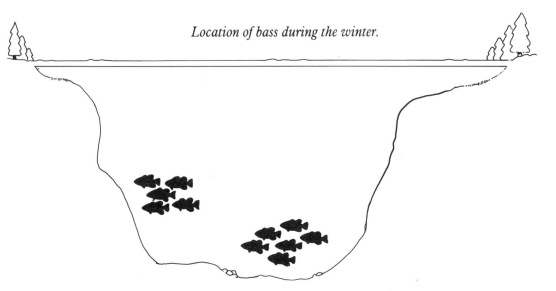

Later in the spring, they move off their beds and start to roam in search of food, comfortable pH, warmth, shelter from enemies and all the other things fish find desirable. They move out gradually, and a good way to look for fish just after spawning is to start along the first breakline (change in depth) in front of their beds, then work your way deeper. If

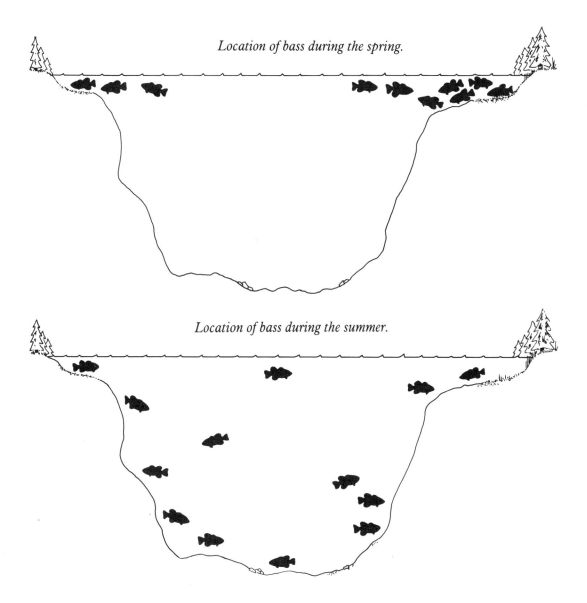

Location of bass during the spring.

Location of bass during the summer.

their beds are in four feet of water, start where the bottom drops off to six feet. Throughout the rest of the summer, you'll find fish in a wide variety of places, depending on local conditions. When temperatures start to drop again in the fall, they'll feed aggressively for a while—stocking up fat for the winter—then begin moving gradually back to deep water again, as the first ice forms in the shallows.

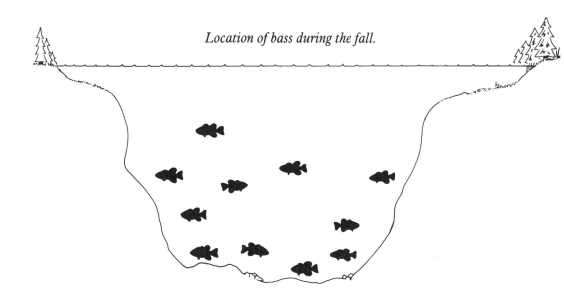

Location of bass during the fall.

Obviously, water temperature is a major factor in the whole cycle, and logical deductions can be made about it. For instance, fish will be more active, earlier in the spring, in spots where the sun shines longer. In some of the hilly regions of Quebec, for example, along the Vermont/New York border, a mountain at the south end of a lake might throw a shadow halfway across the surface most of the day. The north end of that lake, which gets all the sun, is going to warm up quicker every spring, and fish at that end of the lake will start spawning faster than fish at the south end. The seasonal cycles could be several weeks apart at opposite ends of the same lake.

The practical results for the fisherman could be that, at the south end of a lake on a given early-summer day, bass could still be on their beds, not particularly interested in feeding and responding only to slow-presentation baits like jigs. A mile away at the north end, the fish could be actively feeding and ready to take a fast-moving crank or spinnerbait.

Water clarity can have similar effects. In

murky water, for example, light doesn't penetrate as easily, and a murky lake may warm up slower than a clear water one. In clear water, fish may feel more visible—and vulnerable—than they do in a thicker soup. Smallmouth tend to stay in deeper water (even during spawning) in clear lakes than they do in muddy ones.

In addition to seasonal and geographical patterns, there are daily ones, based on weather, availability of food and the rhythms of the fish in a given lake. I've already mentioned how a cold front will slow fish down, and warm weather speed them up again. Storms have effects, too, especially if they're strong enough to start some good wave-action going. Moving water stirs up the bottom, as well as the insects, small fish and other things fish feed on, and consequently it also stirs up bass. Rough water pounding on a point can boil things up enough to get a school of smallmouth really moving, working them into a feeding frenzy where they'll hit anything that moves.

The daily pattern, though, can be fairly steady, especially with schooling fish. In general, it consists of going to the dinner table and coming back, with intervals during which the most recent meal is allowed to settle. In deep lakes and reservoirs, especially where the thermoclines are fairly pronounced, the movement is vertical. Fish will move up to more heavily populated levels to feed on minnows or whatever, and back down to relatively empty areas to rest or suspend. The distances moved depend on where the breaks (changes in temperature, underwater structure, etc.) occur.

I've seen rocky lakes where a long shelf, maybe 50 yards long, juts out and slopes gradually downward to deep water. Smallmouth may suspend in 20 feet of water off the end of the shelf, and move up onto it to feed. They may have to travel 30 or 40 yards each feeding period to get a vertical depth change of 10 or 12 feet. In another spot, the bottom structure may change more quickly, and they may have to move only a yard or so to find their restaurant. In reservoirs, where the bottom structure hardly changes at all, they seem to move up and down with light or temperature changes. Largemouth will do that, too, in reservoirs where they've adjusted to living in deep water and there isn't anything else to relate to. In shallow, weedy lakes, however, like Rice Lake in Ontario, both largemouth and smallmouth tend to move sideways, in and out of weeds, or from one type of weed bed to another.

Whether the movement is vertical or horizontal, though, the point is that it's *repeated*—shifting from one place to feed, to another to rest or suspend—and it's always *related to some kind of break or change*. Spotting the kinds of breaks or changes where fish traffic tends to concentrate is the key to what the pros call "structure fishing," and a sure way to produce consistent catches. Ignoring it is a sure way to come up with nothing.

As already noted, part of the secret of finding fish consists of a process of elimination—looking at a lake or river, deciding which parts are likely to be barren and crossing them off the list right from the start. The barren stretches are usually the ones with little or no structure: for example, deep, open water with a uniform, featureless bottom and no weeds. There isn't any cover or food—no reason for a fish to be there at all. Almost as bad are spots in some glacial lakes where the bottom is all smooth, big, rounded granite boulders, with no vegetation or moss growing on them. Again, there isn't any place for a fish to take shelter or lie in ambush, or for bait fish to school. Smallmouth like rocks, but these boulders are too big and smooth to provide the kind of pockets and crannies crayfish like to hide in. They're a write-off.

SCOUTING THE TERRITORY

Figuring out where the bottom is interesting and where it isn't is a matter of advance scouting. You can never do enough of it, whether you're planning on fishing a lake you've been to 50 times or a brand new one that's as unknown to you as the far side of the moon.

My first step prior to every fishing foray is to pull out the hydrographic charts and pore over them. They show it all, the good, the bad and the ugly, and in minute detail. (You can find charts on sale at local marinas, tackle shops and service stations, or write directly to: Hydrographic Chart Distribution Office, Department of Fisheries and Oceans, P.O. Box 8080, 1675 Russell Road, Ottawa, Ontario K1G 3H6. In the United States, write to: Distribution Branch (N/CG33), National Ocean Service, Riverdale, Maryland 20737.

Every feature of the bottom is marked on these charts: depths, types of bottom material (mud, sand or clay), sunken islands, contour lines, locations of various weed beds, docks, cottages, you name it. Often just knowing the location of a single breakline, where the depth might change three or four feet, can turn out to be the secret of success.

I buy my charts a month or even more before heading out to a new lake, and by the time I get there I just about have the bottom memorized. And that isn't all I do. Sometimes, if there's an airport nearby, I'll hire a pilot for an hour and have him fly me over a lake, to look at it from the air. The cost isn't as high as you'd think—some pilots trying to log hours for a new rating will even take you up just for the price of their aviation gasoline—and the results can be worth it. From the air you can see things that are invisible on the ground: for instance, color changes in weed beds and in the water itself that show variations in depth or species of vegetation. It makes the black lines and numbers on the charts come alive, giving

On any body of water, good fish can be found sitting in ambush around some of the shallow-water boat docks dotting the shoreline. These bass have barely enough water above them to cover their backs. The boat tied to the dock plays a very important role in providing them with homes. The turbulence from the outboard motor's propellor creates a small depression in the bottom, usually three to four feet in diameter, where the boat is docked. A well-placed cast or flip beside the motor and transom can produce some real hogs from these hollows.

When you're on the water, particularly for long periods of time, I highly recommend wearing a pair of polarized fishermen's sunglasses. In addition to taking the glare off the water on bright days, making it more comfortable to stay out all afternoon, these wraparound glasses make it easier to see bottom, minimizing distortion and making underwater features stand out more clearly. With glasses you can spot not only good cover, pockets in weed beds, etc., but also the fish themselves, and know just where to throw a cast.

you an entirely different perspective on what the maps really say.

You may even spot features not marked on the charts—sandbars thrown up by storms in the interval since the most recent charts were printed, humps and bumps the mappers may have missed, sunken boats or fallen-over trees. Ospreys and gulls catch a bellyful of fish every day, remember, and they do it from the air.

An example: There's a sunken boat in one lake I fish now and then, and some pretty hefty smallmouth like to hunker around that old hull. Only a couple of the people in town know about it. Well, one season I went out there and for some reason I just couldn't remember where that hulk was. I racked my brains trying to remember. Was it here, was it there? Finally, I said to heck with it and hired a plane to overfly the lake. Five minutes in the air and I saw the wreck, and when we landed and went out there to fish, the smallies were hitting as hard as ever.

Still another source of information about a lake is the people who live near it. Don't be shy, especially if you're in the local tackle shop and have given the owner your business. Because local people have a stake in keeping visiting anglers happy, they'll frequently give you great tips on where the local lunkers are hiding.

Remember, the main thing you're looking for is changes or transition zones—where the bottom switches from sand to clay, a patch of cabbage weed to coontail, or the depth drops off from five to twenty feet.

Changes on shore are included. For instance, my brother Wayne and I have fished many rivers and reservoirs whose banks look monotonously alike, mile after mile. If there are farms along the shore, however, that's a sure indicator of where the fish are. We just look for the fencerows. Nine times

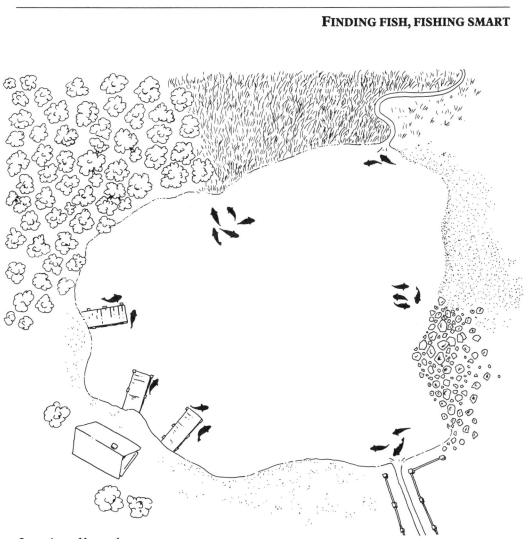

Location of bass along a typical shoreline.

out of ten the farmer put his fence there either because that's where his property ends, and a drainage ditch marks the boundary, or because a stream or creek blocked the way and he couldn't plow any further. Where the ditch or creek comes down to the water, a constant supply of food—insects, plant debris, frogs, etc.—is washed into the main water body, and bait fish will hang around the spot looking for dinner. Where the bait fish are, the bass are, too.

Sometimes we'll just hop from feeder creek to feeder creek, fan-casting around the mouth of each one for a hundred yards or so, and really clean up on smallies.

Of course, finding places where bass are likely to concentrate isn't all there is to angling. Sometimes, despite all logic and common sense, they just aren't there. And even when they are, you still have to catch them. There are so many variables involved that every situation has to be looked at individually—a big pike swimming past, for example, could send the bass scurrying and ruin the most likely of spots.

No book can hope to cover every situation. But here are some of the most typical ones, and how I like to fish them at different seasons.

WEATHER

Outside of season and structure, weather is probably the most important influence on fish behavior. It can shut your fishing right down, or heat it up to the boiling point.

Fronts

We've already noted how a cold front's arrival slows bass down, making them less aggressive (largemouth are more affected than smallmouth, because smallmouth are usually in deeper water where the temperature change doesn't have as sharp an effect). One day you're on a honey hole and they're hitting anything you throw at them, and the next morning they're zombies and won't even look at your lure. A cold front accompanied by wind and cold rain is particularly unfavorable. In a tournament, the only comfort you can take from a cold front's arrival is the knowledge that everybody else has the same problem—the fish aren't any more active for your competitors than they are for you.

But fronts have their good sides, too. I don't really know why, but the day *before* a front arrives fish seem to get super-active. Let the weatherman point at all those lines and squiggles on his map and tell you a front's moving in on Sunday, and you know that Saturday the fishing's likely to be pretty hot. Bass will be very active and hitting your fast-moving lures, so you'll want to get out there and cover a lot of water fast. Use your buzzbaits, spinnerbaits and fast-retrieve crankbaits.

After the cold front moves in, slow down your presentation to suit the altered mood of the fish. If you slayed those largemouth the day before on crankbaits, it's time now to throw your jigs—jig and pig, jig and frog and so forth. If you're not in a tournament situation, where rules forbid it, switch to live baits.

Rain and wind storms

In the summer, rain and wind storms are always coming up, even on warm days, and generally speaking they improve the fishing. On days when there's a bit of a chop on the water, light doesn't penetrate as deeply or easily. It's more diffused, and as a result the fish are less spooky. In addition, the wave motion stirs up the plankton and bottom debris, which gets the bait fish feeding and, inevitably, the predator fish, too. A warm rain produces similar results. The raindrops break up the surface and decrease light penetration, while the water running off the shore and out feeder creeks stirs up debris, insects and plankton. The fish are more confident and more active. They also tend to disperse over a wider area rather than bunching up and holding in one spot. Whenever it's raining or blowing, I use reaction-type baits—spinnerbaits and crankbaits—casting along the wave trough and covering lots of water.

Hot summer days

Fish like warmth, which speeds them up, but they also have to protect their eyes from too much light, and so on a real scorcher they'll try to escape light penetration. Largemouth will head for shade—

boat docks, broad-leafed lily pads and so forth—while smallmouth will drop back into deeper water, where the sun's rays have farther to travel to reach them. They'll both be tighter to cover on such days, but will still hit a wide variety of lures. They have the energy to go after crankbaits, but rather than trying to cover a large area, fan-casting and cranking, concentrate on patches of shady cover, throwing just beyond them and reeling your bait back past the spot.

The way bass react to weather is all very logical, when you think about it. Of course, logic can take some bizarre turns, especially when people get involved in the process and make their own artificial "weather." Once, at a tournament in Florida, I watched the effect of boat wakes on largemouth in a narrow canal, and it was the same as in a heavy rainstorm. The canal ran between two big lakes and guys were running through there all day in bass boats with big, "buck and a half" 150-horse motors on them, washing up waves on the banks. I was working the shoreline with plastic worms, and the fish were so tuned-in to those boats that the majority of my strikes came when a boat was going past. The wave action would roil up the water, making it murky, and wash debris, insects and clods of dirt down off the banks into the canal. I'd toss a worm in just as that happened and, bang, there was a fish.

I got so excited over it that the guys were kidding me. A friend of mine, Basil Bacon, came roaring up at 60 mph, took his boat off plane and let this huge wave come washing across. His partner was hanging over the side of the boat, pretending to push the water at me. They knew how I was fishing. But the pattern was there. I think the bass were actually reacting to the sound of the passing motors, gauging how long after one passed a wave would hit, and waiting for some goodies to flop down into the water. I had a sort of artificial storm going for me.

Bass congregating around various types of underwater structure and cover.

WATER BODIES

Obviously how you fish also depends a great deal on where you fish. The basic type of water you have to work with decides a lot of things, right from the start. Here's how I approach some typical water body types.

Shallow, weedy lakes

These are ideal largemouth waters, although they'll hold some big smallmouth as well. The first place to try in early season, of course, is in shallow water just off the shore areas where fish have been spawning. As already noted, after spawning smallmouth will start dropping back into deeper water, moving from the first breakline to the second and on out, but largemouth—especially in lakes where there isn't a lot of deep water anyway—tend to drop back into denser cover. There may be a largemouth bed in two feet of water across from a dock. After spawning, the male will stay on the nest, but the female may swim off under the dock, or to a nearby patch of thick weeds, looking for shade and the security of a physical feature to which she can relate. I caught one like that under a dock in a July tournament, a four-pound hen with the tail still bleeding. Obviously, she'd just come off the bed, illustrating the fact that there are early spawners and late spawners.

In mid-season, fish are widely dispersed, scattered all over the weed flats and every other part of the lake. But there are some spots where finding them is a little easier. For example, a good location for largemouth would be the edges of the deeper weed lines. Look on the map for those big, wide bays that almost seem to have "Big Jaws" written on them, and head out to the farthest weed edge of that bay, bordering deeper water. The bay might average two or three feet in depth most of the way out, then break into six and then ten, twelve, and fifteen feet. When you find that last weed line before the deepest water, work right along its edge, looking for some feature that stands out. It may be an inside turn, a point in the weeds, an underwater funnel running like a submerged creekbed through the weeds, or maybe a change in the species of weeds growing there, from milfoil and coontail to cabbage weed. That's where the largemouth will be waiting. You can pull a crankbait past there, parallel with the weed line, or work the unusual feature itself with a plastic worm or a jig. Frequently, if I'm fishing, say, a weed line where it breaks from six feet into ten feet of water, I'll use a $3/8$-ounce bullethead with a six- to seven-inch plastic worm, or even a jig and pig. You can either stay off the edge, keeping your boat about ten feet away from the weed edge, and cast straight into the spots that look good, or work your worm parallel to the line. Either way, you stand a good chance of getting a largemouth to bang your lure.

Landing a smallie caught on a spinnerbait in pencil reeds.

◀🐟◀ Working weed beds, especially lily pads and reeds, make sure you use a fairly heavy line, and either a heavy-action bait-casting rod or a flipping rod for strength and leverage in ripping through the cover.

On the weed flats themselves, where isolated fish are scattered here, there and everywhere, the idea is to cover the widest possible area as quickly as you can. A good locating lure for this type of work is a buzzbait, or a big willow leaf spinnerbait, number seven or eight, that thumps along and makes vibrations. Move along quickly, fan-casting all around the boat, until you get a hit. Sometimes bass will hit at a buzzbait and miss. It's a big lure, moving fast with a lot of splashing, and they can misjudge their lunge. If that happens, follow up on the missed strike by throwing a plastic worm to the fish. Sometimes I've really cleaned up that way. Other good lures in weed flat situations are the safety-pin-design spinnerbaits, especially those with a living rubber skirt. They make a lot of commotion running just under the surface, or half-in, half-out of the water, and their design prevents them from tangling on weeds. Another "old reliable" is the traditional bucktail spinner, such as the Mepps spinner, the bucktail of which seems to keep the hook from getting caught in the weeds.

During late season on shallow lakes, look for the same features you'd seek in mid-season, but also pay attention to the state of the weeds. The best place to fish is where the weeds are still green, rather than areas where they've turned brown and started to die off. Dying, decomposing weeds use up oxygen and, while some fish will loiter near them, you'll find much better pickings where the vegetation is still alive. In the fall, I'll often fish weed lines that are still green with a plastic worm, rigged Texas-style.

Flipping under the root systems of reeds.

Deep, rocky lakes

These are another case entirely. Just as the shallow lakes are prime largemouth territory, deep lakes are where Little Jaws likes to roam.

In early season, immediately after spawning, you'll find both largemouth and smallmouth in the shallow areas, around shallow coves and just off points. But it can be pretty tough fishing in these colder lakes at this time of year, because post-spawn fish can be very lethargic. For smallmouth, try the first breakline or two just out from the spawning grounds, where the bottom drops from five to eight feet or from five to twelve feet. Also check the edges of any shoal areas, where the bottom just starts to drop off into deeper water, or the first break on the edge of a sunken island or underwater hump. For largemouth, look for cover, even sparse cover. There may not be many weeds in these lakes, compared to the lush beds in shallow, muddy lakes, but if there is any cover at all, Big Jaws will head for it. Even a tiny patch of weeds, up near shore, could hold largemouth. In general, this is the time of year to work the shorelines, moving around the lake's perimeter and banging your lure in there at all the likely spots.

Post-spawn smallmouth may respond to jigs at this time of year, while largemouth may go for a jig or plastic worm.

In mid-season, you'll still want to orient yourself toward shore, for the simple reason that in the very deep, glacial lakes—typical lake trout territory with centers that may drop down a hundred feet or more—the only place for bass to be is along shore. But you can move out a bit farther now, away from the first breakline and into deeper water. You'll find smallmouth relating to breaklines and rock structures in 15, 20 or 30 feet of water, where they'll often suspend in schools between feeding periods. Fish for them with deep-diving, crayfish-colored crankbaits, and jigs. It helps to look for their food, spots where broken rock provides hiding places for crayfish. Look especially for spots that combine a food source with nearby deep water. Rocky shelves that slant down into the depths are ideal, providing the forage is nearby.

In the later part of the season when it's starting

to get cold again, bait fish are no longer abundant in the shallow areas onshore, where the water may already be freezing over at night. They move deeper, and the predators follow. The place to look for smallmouth then is on the deeper breaklines around shoals and underwater humps. For largemouth, cast on the deep side of the outer weed lines.

A characteristic of fall fishing is the tendency of fish to school up very tightly. There can be two people in a boat, casting opposite sides, and one will get all the fish. It's incredible how tight and precise a school can be. I've seen cases in deep water where, if you didn't cast within a three-foot-diameter circle, you wouldn't catch a fish—not one. But if you kept hitting that little area, you could limit out.

Big, fast-moving rivers

Rivers like the St. Lawrence present another kind of challenge. Largemouth and smallmouth have different preferences in these rivers, with largemouth favoring whatever shallow, slow water can be found and smallmouth seeking the deeper spots and stronger current.

Look for largemouth in large, still-water expanses that may be created by a back eddy off a breakwall, a bend in the river that slows the current down, the lee of a big sandbar or in the heavy weed growth right along shore. You'll find smallmouth in much smaller sheltered patches right out in the current—sitting behind a single rock, for example, or a rock crib or a group of deep pilings. They won't be directly in the current, but sheltered behind a smaller obstacle near it. I've caught smallmouth in these pockets in current where my boat was drifting so fast I'd travel 40 yards downstream between each cast.

Remember, fish always face in the direction the current is coming from, and your lure has to pass in front of, rather than behind them, if you want them to get a good look at it. Cast up-current, beyond the cover where you think there are fish, and bring your lure back downstream past them. Smallmouth waiting behind a rock will dart out into the current to hit your bait, then scoot back to cover with it. If you cast behind the spot, the fish may not see your bait, or worse yet, you may drop your line right into their ambush spot, hit one on the tail and spook it. Also remember, when fishing in strong current, that it doesn't look very natural for a bait to be moving 100 mph *against* the current. It would have to be some kind of Super Minnow to do that. Cast across the current, or against it, and reel back fairly slowly to make it look natural. Cast with the current and reel back against it like a windmill, and the fish will know there's something fishy!

Still another characteristic of fast-moving rivers is the here-today-gone-tomorrow quality of the fishing. Probably because of the current itself, fish seem to roam all over the place, schooling up in a group of shallow boulders one day, and traveling 1,000 yards downstream to entirely different cover the next. Smallmouth are especially unreliable in this kind of environment and competitive fishing under big-river conditions can be unpredictable.

Wide, calm, slow-moving rivers

These often provide some of the best largemouth fishing there is. One big, sluggish river I've worked has a five-mile stretch that largemouth must think is heaven, because they all want to go there. We took 48 pounds, 5 ounces of fish—twelve bass—out of it in one tournament, and I'm sure we only saw the tip of the iceberg. The current was so slow it was almost non-existent.

These kinds of rivers are especially productive where the banks are undercut and lined on either side with cattails and bullrushes or overhanging willows. On sunny days in mid-season, bass will sit under the banks for shade, waiting for something tasty to slide down into the water, and you can nail them by flipping plastic worms tight to the banks. On overcast days, the fish will roam more, but they still tend to loiter around the edges of the shoreline, in the weeds, where you can pick them off with a variety of lures, including spinnerbaits and crankbaits.

Some slow-moving rivers also have little bays with lily pads in them, or fallen-over trees, and these are good spots for bass. Generally, you'll find more largemouth when the water is murky or muddy, and smallmouth where it's relatively clear. Remember when fishing from a boat in these rivers to stay out some distance from shore and cast toward the banks, rather than moving close along the shoreline where your boat's shadow and the sound of the motor or oars can spook fish.

River mouths

River mouths can be real hot spots, because of the food that flows out on the current and attracts fish. For smallmouth, I'll try any points that jut out into the river mouth, working the deeper breaklines and looking for rocks or weed clumps that might provide small islands to hide behind in the current. For largemouth, I'll flip to the banks, especially if they're undercut. As a general rule, look for the first cover available near the spot where the river intersects the bigger body of water.

Swamps and flooded cedar or tamarack stands

These aren't as common in Canada as they are in the United States, but you run into them now and then, and some hold their share of bass. Finding lunkers in a big swamp, however, can be a real problem. It's the same kind of situation as in a big weed flat: there's so much good cover that the fish could be scattered anywhere. It's difficult to know

Fishing a flooded treeline in a reservoir.

where to start. When I have to fish this sort of place, I try to work a lot of water quickly, with buzzbaits or spinnerbaits, or just isolate a portion of it and explore only that. Sometimes, if the trees have only recently been flooded and it's still green around the edges, I'll fish shallow. Largemouth seem to like to come up into the green stuff in newly flooded areas.

If it's a small swamp, I'll fish it thoroughly, but a really wide expanse is too much to handle and the best you can do is to give it a once-over. The key is to look for something a little different, some unusual feature.

Canals

Canals, particularly placid, muddy ones, are a little like swamps in that they have a surplus of good cover and hold some really big fish. On a hot summer day in mid-season, I like to move down them using the electric motor and flipping to floating logs, willow overhangs, lily pads, deadheads and so forth. Canals lined with cottages and houses are often largemouth hangouts. Boat-houses, docks and breakwalls should be worked as potential spots. Smallmouth can be found in canals providing there is some current, but they are primarily largemouth waters.

INDIVIDUAL FEATURES

Points

Points come in all types and sizes, from weed points formed by the growth patterns of plants underwater, to small rock points, full-blown natural peninsulas and man-made breakwalls and causeways. One thing they all have in common, however, is that fish love them. They're ambush spots for them, where the bait fish are plentiful and they can lie in wait in good cover, sheltered from the current. I've won several tournaments simply by point-hopping, moving around a lake and fishing as many as 20 or 30 points in a day.

Points in general, including rocks, weeds and shoals, can be magnets for both smallmouth and largemouth.

Before approaching a point, I like to check over the hydrographic charts and see how things look down there to the fish. The chart will show where the breaklines are, whether there are boulders (these are indicated by little X's) and where the vegetation is. Sometimes where a field of weeds narrows to a point, because the soil composition or something else has changed in that spot, you'll find a honey hole.

After looking at the chart, I check the water color, whether it's clear or murky. If it's clear, I'll start in deep water and work my way shallow, casting ahead so that I've covered the area before my boat passes over and spooks the fish. I'll try first in the water straight off the point, 15 feet or deeper, where a crankbait couldn't get down, tossing a jig for smallmouth or a living rubber jig and pork or a plastic worm for largemouth. I'll work these slowly, then move up closer to shore and try either my deep-diving crankbaits or controlled-depth, sinking-type baits like a Spot, that go down a foot and a half per second. Finally, I'll move right up into shallow water and work my topwater lures—buzzbaits and poppers—or maybe twitch a Redfin or some other pencil plug. This sequence—starting off the tip of the point and working from deep to shallow—lets me cover the whole area thoroughly without scaring off the fish.

If you want to reverse the process and begin in shallow water, come in close to shore some distance to the left or right of the point itself and move up on it slowly and quietly from the side. As you work your way out to deep water, keep your boat far enough offshore to avoid spooking your quarry. An electric motor is ideal for this kind of situation.

In murky water you don't have to be quite so worried about spooking fish, and chances are you won't have to go as deep to find them, either. Remember, smallmouth stay closer to the surface in colored water than they do where it's clear. I usually

➤When dealing with points on a windy day, try the rough water side first. The wave action on the windward side will stir up the bottom and the plankton and get fish feeding more actively than they'd be on the lee side.

start in about fifteen feet and "rattle the point" with a noisy, deep-diving rattler crankbait. Then I'll move into shallower water and try a spinnerbait, preferably one with a large blade to get a lot of thump and flash, or else a buzzbait. I don't bother with other types of plugs because they don't make enough commotion, and commotion is what you want in the murky stuff.

Riprap, rock cribs, breakwalls and other man-made obstructions

Look for these features. On a multi-species lake you'll find both largemouth and smallmouth. Riprap and broken concrete hold the crayfish that attract smallies, but they also break the current, and provide shade and structure for fish to relate to when weeds are sparse. Rondeau Bay on Lake Erie is a good example. The weeds that were there when I was a kid are gone now, and the fish relate to the breakwalls and riprap instead. A square concrete breakwall, of course, won't cast a shadow very far, so there isn't a lot of point in fishing more than five feet away from it, unless there are broken rocks or boulders continuing out under the water, where fish can find food. The way to fish a smooth breakwall is to cast a crankbait or worm parallel to it, a foot or so out from the edge. The constant wave action along the wall will scoop out a small depression at the bottom, and fish seem to like to hang around there. Water will scoop out spots in riprap, too, and they're sometimes good spots to find largemouth.

You have to use a little common sense fishing riprap. For example, in shallow areas where the rocks are in water only two feet deep or so, the fishing wouldn't be worth a hoot on a windy day. The waves beating against them would batter any bass that tried to hold there up against the rocks. On a flat, calm day, though, the same spot might be full of fish.

Flipping a boat dock. The best docks to fish are low to the water, made of wood and provide lots of shade for Old Bucketmouth.

Docks and boat-houses

These are a key feature on any lake, especially in mid-season when the sun beats down on the water, and in clear lakes where the light penetrates easily. Largemouth, especially, look for shade on a sunny day and are often found lurking under a dock. The ones they like best are those that provide structure as well as shade—older wooden docks with thick wooden pilings on which moss and algae have had plenty of time to grow. Floating docks may occasionally hold fish, but with no pilings underneath they offer only a bit of shade and no structure. The same is true of docks with steel girder pilings, which are thinner than wooden ones and don't provide a good surface where weeds and moss can cling. You may catch a fish under there now and then, but not as many as you will near an old-fashioned wooden dock.

The way I like to work both docks and boat-houses is to approach very quietly, drifting past them slowly and well back from the spot I want to try, so as not to give my presence away. Then I'll take a good, old black plastic worm and cast it first to the tip of the dock—drawing it past parallel to the end—and then, if that doesn't produce a hit, I'll toss a cast on each side of the dock. Sometimes I'll even tease the fish, tossing the worm up onto the dock itself and giving it a little tug so it flops down into the water right off the dock surface. If you're in a hurry and there are several docks in the vicinity, you can cover them a little faster using a spinnerbait, but nothing really beats those old black worms.

Weed flats

As already noted, weed flats can be difficult places to find fish because of the overabundance of cover; they could be anywhere in that submerged jungle. Nevertheless, these are terrific places to look and shouldn't be neglected just because they're hard

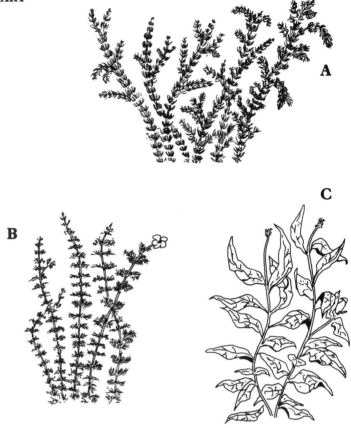

Aquatic weeds: (A) coontail; (B) milfoil; (C) cabbage weed.

🐟 Where weeds are concerned, you'll be surprised at the size of tuft that will attract fish. If there isn't any other cover around, even a handful of pencil reeds will hold a bass. Fish need something, anything, to relate to and, to them, even five or six thin stems are apparently better than nothing. Don't pass them up.

to deal with. I've seen several tournaments won by guys who "fished the flats." The best approach is to fish economically, covering as much surface area as possible as quickly as you can. I recommend using either a buzzbait or a safety-pin-type spinnerbait. It's also a good idea to keep your boat moving along as you cast.

While you move through the flats, look for lines where patches of weeds end, or the species composition changes. Fish will often concentrate there. The outside line of the flat, where the weeds stop, is also a good producer. I zig-zag across these, hitting first the shallow side, then the deep, then the shallow again, or else I just move along the line and work my lure parallel to it. If I find fish this way using a crankbait or spinnerbait, I'll sometimes follow up by working that spot more thoroughly with a jig or worm.

Of course, you can't talk about weeds without talking about lily pads. As cover they're sometimes overrated, but they do produce bass, especially largemouth. Rather than cruise through huge fields of them, I like to look for isolated patches ten or even five feet in diameter, or tiny clumps of three or four pads, off by themselves in otherwise empty water. On sunny days, these will hold fish, lurking under them for the shade.

An assortment of lily pads and other aquatic cover can hide a good number of large-mouth.

A northern pike and a small-mouth bass caught on the same weed line. The small-mouth weighs close to five pounds. A bass that will mingle with pike or muskie under the same cover will generally be larger than nor-mal. Any smaller and it would be dinner.

My favorite lure for lily pads is a weedless spoon with wire weed-guards and a living rubber skirt. I tie it onto my line with a split ring to give it more wobble, and sometimes put a trailer hook on it, too, for good measure. I cast the spoon over the patch of pads and beyond it, reel in and work it up the far side, onto a pad, then pull it over and let it fall off on the near side and flutter down. I've seen bass, at that point, just blow right up through the pads like missiles, smashing the spoon. If you're not expecting it, it can scare the heck out of you. Other times, they'll be sneaky about it and suck the spoon in so quietly that you don't even notice at first that they've taken it. Bass! They're unpredictable.

The best colors for spoons are white, chrome, gold and black. I use chrome in murky water, white or gold in clear water and black in clear water on overcast days.

Islands

Whether they're made of reeds, rocks or man-made concrete, islands attract fish. Of course, very large islands, such as Amherst or Wolfe islands near Kingston, Ontario, are large enough to be treated as if they were a mainland shore. You approach them the same way you'd approach any shore, looking for points, bays and so on and fishing the individual features. Smaller islands, however, have their own characteristics.

An island small enough for you to zip around with your electric motor in a few minutes can be a real honey hole. Reed or cattail islands are dynamite spots for largemouth. Pencil reed patches are wonderful for smallmouth in early season, and later on the largemouth move into them. I've won a number of tournaments fishing both kinds of places. For example, a reed island 50 by 30 feet in the middle of a big bay may be loaded with largemouth. When I find a location like that, I first fish the edges with spinnerbaits, then get into the thick stuff with a plastic worm or a jig and pig, sometimes flipping my lure 30 feet back into them. A variation on the reed island is the floating reed mat, under which bass sometimes like to hide. A good way to fish these is to toss a jig over top of it and shake it until it slips down through the mat and into the water. Then, using your line and the edge of the mat, see-saw that jig up and down slowly. It's a method that pays off.

Another type of weed island is the pencil reed thicket, which is common in Lake St. Clair. Early in the season, smallmouth will frequently stage there just after spawning, on their way out to deeper

On sunny days use the flipping technique to produce some real hogs from around duck blinds.

A partly submerged tree is a likely spot for a fish or two.

water. Try them with crayfish-colored crankbaits, chrome-bladed or white spinnerbaits, and buzzbaits. If you think largemouth might be using the pencil reeds for cover, hit them with spinnerbaits with big, willow-leaf blades, for example number sevens, or work a plastic worm through them slowly.

As for rocky islands, the best way to cover them is first to work the points, starting up near shore and moving gradually out to where a deep-diving crankbait or Spot-type lure can be used, and finally into the deep water with a jig.

Deadheads and willow overhangs

These small features are great places to find fish, especially old Big Jaws. If you're cruising along a canal or bay, or a slow river with murky water, and spot a deadhead floating, toss a spinner or a crankbait just beyond it and reel it back past the spot. You may get a major league hit. If there's a deadfall or low-overhanging tree on the bank, especially an undercut bank, try a plastic worm.

Sandbars

A bit like islands, sandbars are frequent schooling spots, where fish of roughly similar size like to hang around, cruising for forage. Sometimes you'll see all kinds of boils and swirls on the surface, and you know the largemouth are schooling there. Your best bet if they're active is to use crankbaits and start cracking. Once you've taken off the most aggressive fish on a sandbar, you can go to jigs, plastic worms or live bait to take off the rest.

If the bar is shallow, I work the edges first and move toward deeper water, but only rarely will I bother to work the tips. It's good to keep in mind, too, that fish on sandbars will move around on you. They cruise more when they're in a school, and if you tune into one, you'll have to follow it as you fish. Keep your boat off the bar about ten or twenty yards so that you don't spook them, and move slowly in the direction you think they're going.

Sand beaches and gravel beaches

In the daytime, sand beaches are generally not the best spots to fish, especially if swimmers or water skiers are nearby. Because sand is often bare of vegetation and provides no screen from the sun, bait fish avoid these open stretches when it's light. Night fishing, however, is another story. Frequently the bait fish are out on the sand flats when it's dark, and the predators cruise around them as if they were in a restaurant. My friend Gary Burghoff, who played Radar on the old "M.A.S.H." television series, caught a smallmouth that might have been a state record on a sand beach in Connecticut one night, using a big black Jitterbug. The fish weighed-in at 6.9 pounds after a week in the freezer. I caught a five-pounder not far from there myself, working a jig in the daytime near a floating barrel raft.

Gravel beaches are a similar proposition. During the daytime, they're generally not the best place to find fish, even though they may attract a few smallies looking for crayfish. The best time to fish them is at night. If you have to fish there during the day, work the line just off the end of the gravel, where it breaks into deeper water.

Mudlines

Breaklines don't always take the form of a change in depth or vegetation. Sometimes you get a change in water clarity that's sharp enough to be called a mudline. A frequent example is a spot where a muddy river or canal empties into an otherwise clear lake. Or it could be caused by rain water runoff from a clay bank after a heavy storm. Whatever the cause, right where the clear water meets the muddy water you can catch fish—especially if there isn't any other attractive cover nearby and the line is the only thing they have to relate to. The way to work them is to cast something noisy like a rattling crankbait or a big spinnerbait that really thumps along, putting it right on the dividing line itself, and then reel in parallel to the line.

Road culverts

These attract fish, especially if the water on one side of the culvert is relatively calm and the water on the opposite side has some current to it. A dike, with a deep canal opposite, is a prime example. There's one like that near Rondeau Bay, and it always holds fish on one side or the other. Watch on days when the wind is blowing and water is being forced through the culvert. The bass—and every other fish around—will stack up on the side the water is being blown toward. If the wind shifts, they'll move to the other side. I've caught as many as a dozen bass just casting on the correct side.

"Burnt-out" lakes and virgin lakes

Lakes that have been fished so heavily that you'd swear nothing could be left, or ones that seem almost totally undiscovered, provide the angler with two distinctly different kinds of challenge.

The most difficult is probably the former. It can throw you for a loop to sail out onto a lake in, say, the Muskokas, with prime bass cover everywhere, try all the obvious spots and come up with absolutely zip. You begin to wonder if your mind isn't going, or if acid rain has wiped out all the fish in the lake. But the only problem is familiarity. Any lunkers still swimming around out there have seen it all. They know the serial numbers on every lure, and you just can't catch them by going the obvious route.

In a case like that, a good bet is to try the heaviest cover first. When a lot of fishermen and boats are out there every day, the bass get driven off their favorite spots and have to retreat to the second-choice areas. Instead of holding on a weed line, they'll drop back deep into the weeds, or move to other cover that isn't being fished so much. For instance, sunken islands and underwater humps aren't visible to the naked eye. Only fishermen equipped with a depth-finder are going to know where they are, so they're fished less intensively. On a lake with a lot of traffic, I'll look for smallmouth on deep humps way out in the middle of the lake, with centers around 20 to 25 feet deep and edges breaking off into 40 to 50 feet of water. You can fish these with jigs and make a nice haul while everybody else is wasting time in places the whole world has already worked over. Other good spots are busy boat docks and marinas that fishermen just assume won't hold anything. Sometimes you can throw a cast by a dock with a group of sunbathers sitting on one side and haul a largemouth out on the other.

Besides looking in obscure places, it's also a good idea to try different lure presentations. In a heavily fished area, I'm not likely to use a buzzbait or a lot of flashy attention-getters. The fish have been watching them go by all day and they only make them yawn. A better approach is to try a super-slow presentation. If a spot looks good, "dead-stick" a worm there. Cast it in and just let it sit for a long while. Then lift it up slowly, shake it a bit, and let it flutter down again. Don't rush, just take your time. A wary fish may watch that worm lie there for quite a while, then finally decide it's safe and suck it in. Of course, it goes without saying that a live worm will work better in this type of lake than a plastic one. As a general rule, live bait will always draw better in a heavily fished lake than artificial lures will.

It also pays to keep trying a likely spot even if you don't get a hit on the first cast or two. In a burnt-out lake, you have to be a little like the persistent encyclopedia salesman who won't take his foot out of the door. The day before one tournament I was in, one of the other contestants caught a nice four-pounder during a practice session and released it. The next day, when the tournament was on, he went back to that same dock and just kept flipping to it until he caught it again. It took him about seventeen flips, until the fish couldn't stand it anymore and hit.

Also, like sandy beaches, heavily fished lakes produce better at night than they do in the daytime. When it gets dark, fishing pressure usually eases off, and those wary bass will feel safe and come out to feed. Topwater lures—Tiny Torpedos, Zara-Spooks, poppers, pencil plugs that you can twitch on the surface, and so forth—can clean up for you in these conditions.

Rocky bluffs are smallmouth habitats. Try fishing tight to the bluff using a crankbait or a jig.

As for those rare, untouched lakes that seem never to have been fished by a hog-hunter, you'll think you're in heaven if you find one. I've fished some lakes in the Maritimes, where smallmouth until recently were considered trash fish (what an insult!) and thought some diver down there was tying fish onto my line. They can be tricky, though, if you're used to fishing tougher waters. There's a tendency to sail past obvious spots, saying to yourself, "Heck, that's too easy. Everybody must have tried it." But in reality they haven't. I fish a fresh lake in almost the exact opposite way that I fish a burnt-out spot, using fast-moving plugs and hitting the traditional places first: shallow breaklines, shallow rocky points, the most visible weeds.

And all the time I'm doing it I'll have a big grin on my face.

SEVEN   BASS BOATS

I've fished for bass from some odd places, including the little, $25 eight-footer that big fish used to tow me in as a youngster on Rondeau Bay. Other people have used even stranger tubs, from rubber rafts to sailboats and (for all I know) kayaks. The fact is, a lumberjack might be able to catch a bass while dancing on a log. But there are easier ways, and more practical boats.

The most practical boats for bassing, of course, are the high-performance bass boats used by pros in tournament competition. Everything on my own 18-foot, fiberglass-hulled Ranger, from the 150-horsepower V-6 outboard on the transom to the 28-pound, foot-pedal-controlled electric thruster mounted in the bow, is geared specifically toward giving its owner the competitive edge in going after two fish: Big Jaws and Little Jaws. These boats have become commonplace in the United States, where some individual dealers may sell as many as 400 or 500 boats per year, and they're becoming a trend in Canada, as well.

But not everybody needs top-of-the-line equipment, nor can every weekender afford the price tag. Most anglers' needs will likely fall somewhere between the extremes represented by my first boat and my latest one and, as in buying tackle, common sense should prevail.

Here are some points to keep in mind when you go shopping for a boat.

Bob's 150-horse-power, 18-foot bass boat.

WATER TYPE AND WALLET SIZE

The first question to consider is what kind of waters you'll be fishing. If you plan on spending most of your time on small, sheltered lakes, farm ponds, quiet swamps, feeder creeks or small rivers, there's no real reason to invest in an aircraft carrier. An old-fashioned, flat-bottom Johnboat, a wide-beam duckboat or even a fairly wide-beam canoe can serve your purpose quite well. They can also save you money, on both the purchase price and the built-in economy of owning a multi-use craft.

If you intend to fish broad, fast-current rivers or larger lakes where storms can whip up a respectable chop, you'll want something bigger and more stable. The traditional, 15- to 18-foot aluminum V-bottom, designed for running with a 35- to 50-horsepower outboard, has been a fixture on the Great Lakes and adjacent waters for years, and provides a dependable, solid platform for the basser who sometimes finds himself in rougher water. Built more for sit-down, rather than stand-up casting, they also have a bit of wind resistance because of their higher freeboards. But they're good for fishing a variety of species, not just bass, and their higher sides and transoms do make them more secure against waves than a Johnboat—and practical for back-trolling, as well. Recently, a variation of this type of boat has been introduced that features flat, rather than sloping, floors and pedestal seats similar to those used in pro bass boats. A keen basser with a lean bankroll who frequently goes after walleye, pike or other fish would find this design just about ideal.

Another consideration is the number of people who'll likely be fishing from the boat you buy. For two men, a 15-footer is adequate, but for three or more a 17- or 18-foot craft is required. Safety should be your prime concern on the water, and an overloaded boat is the most dangerous thing afloat.

The extremely stable modern bass boat is designed for stand-up fishing. It can also be used for water skiing.

If you decide to fish in high gear with the ultimate fishing machine, one that can move you from hot spot to honey hole fast, a high-performance boat is an absolute necessity. In tournaments, when your competitors are capable of running at 60-plus mph between fishing spots, you want to be able to keep up to have the best chance of making back your entry fees. Besides speed, a boat designed for tournaments has all sorts of invaluable features: a flat deck for easy on-board movement; removable bow and aft platform seats for convenient casting and wider observation of the waters around your boat; compact, safe storage compartments for your tackle and extra rods and reels (enclosed so they won't blow or bounce overboard when you're running full out), and built-in wiring systems capable of hosting a wide variety of electronic equipment, from depth-sounders to surface temperature gauges.

BASS BOATS

A foot-controlled electric motor can keep your hands free for fishing. The small bicycle-style seat in bass boats is used to give the fisherman stability to work the electric motor. It also allows you to keep your concentration without getting too comfortable.

The tournament crowd spend hours yakking about the pros and cons of such boats and their myriad optional features, and everyone has an opinion about everything, from the best type of battery to power a thruster to the best color of metal-flake striping for a hull. Cost is almost impossible to give advice on, because prices and models change so frequently, and the value of second-hand boats is so subjective, that anything I might say here could be outdated the day after it appears in print. At the very least, it would prompt several hundred catcalls, snorts of derision, chuckles and comments to the effect that: "That Izumi really *is* full of it, isn't he?" All I'll venture to say on this score is: buy from a reputable dealer, insist on a good warranty and use your head.

DON'T SKIMP

Whichever brand or style of bass boat you choose, I'd recommend that you not skimp on equipment (if you have to, you probably shouldn't be purchasing this type of boat in the first place), but that you outfit your baby with at least the following instrumentation: an in-dash depth-finder, tachometer, water pressure gauge, trim gauge, gas gauge (sounds obvious, but it isn't always standard), voltmeter and surface temperature gauge.

Also, despite the claims of some people who may consider it unnecessary or "wimpy," get a kill switch. Designed to attach to the operator's body when running, this device will automatically shut off your engine in the event you are bounced or tossed overboard, thus ensuring that your uncontrolled boat will not turn in a circle and run over you. Major manufacturers are providing these as standard equipment on many models, but not all older boats have them. If you purchase a used high-performance boat and it hasn't got a kill switch, I'd advise you to put one in it yourself. We hog-hunters like to catch fish, not feed them.

Of course, it goes without saying that good, basic boating safety is part of the furniture that ought to occupy a basser's brain. It wouldn't hurt to take a course in small craft handling and boating safety before you start fishing on the bigger lakes, and to learn the regulations governing small boat navigation on inland waterways. The rules—from the requirement to carry a flotation device for every person aboard to the elementary good sense of checking to see that your running lights are working before leaving on an overnight trip—are there to protect you, not annoy you.

No fish is worth the risk of drowning.

EIGHT

CATCH-AND-RELEASE FISHING

A U.S. fishing pro once remarked that a good bass is "too important to only be caught once." He was speaking in the aesthetic sense, appreciating the species' fighting qualities, but what he said is true in a literal sense, too. The fact is, with the rapid destruction of bass habitat by acid rain, chemical waste dumping and the endless expansion of our industrial farm and factory system, as well as the rising pressure of an ever-greater number of sport fishermen, the bass populations in some parts of Canada and the United States are being harmed. The value of the individual, fighting bass is appreciating just like any other scarce commodity.

Over-fishing alone can do a surprising amount of damage. I've seen some prime spots burned out in a week, and it bothers me to think that, if nobody does anything about it, a day could come when the thrill of catching a real lunker in the five-pound-plus range will be a statistical impossibility for most anglers.

Fortunately, there's something we can do about it. In addition to supporting the efforts of environmentalists to stop pollution and habitat destruction, we can relieve the pressure on our local bass populations and take out our own bass insurance policies by practising the fine art of catch-and-release fishing.

This may sound like a strange notion at first, and many people have a hard time understanding

Wayne Izumi carefully releases a smallmouth.

why anyone would go to all the trouble of catching a fish he didn't plan to keep. But it's a very logical response to the present situation. After all, bass anglers fish primarily for sport, not food. If all a fisherman wanted was a meal, he could get a much cheaper one at the fish market than by spending hundreds of dollars on a boat, tackle and road trips all over the landscape. As for proving one's prowess, bringing home a stringer full of dead fish isn't necessary to do that. You can get the same effect at lakeside, with a camera. Personally, I've caught thousands of bass, but I haven't actually kept one in at least five years.

Don't get me wrong. I'm not some kind of Fish Rights extremist who thinks anyone who eats his catch is "a barbarian involved in a nauseating blood sport" (a British animal rights advocate once actually wrote that in a magazine). I'm just saying there's no need to keep every fish you net that measures over the legal length limit.

It's a matter of selection and moderation. If you've been on the water all morning and are looking forward to a fresh-caught shore lunch, two fish will fill up the normal stomach. If there are five in your livewell, why not let the other three go? Unless one of them is that once-in-a-lifetime, record wall-hanger you just *have* to have mounted, there's really no logical reason to keep them all. Increasingly, true sportsmen are coming to see it that way—all of the fish caught in professional bass tournaments are released alive after weigh-in. (There's even a case to be made for not keeping trophy-sized bass, on the grounds that the biggest fish are the most successful feeders, fighters and breeders and should be preserved to pass their genes to future generations.)

SIMPLE MECHANICS

The mechanics of catch-and-release are fairly simple, especially with largemouth bass, whose jaws

A couple of largemouth about to be released at a tournament.

are strong enough to allow the fisherman to "lip" them while removing a hook. With "toothy critters" like pike or walleye, this process would be hard on the fingers, and other species' jaws would be injured by it, but bass seem unaffected. After bringing your fish to the boat, simply grasp its lower jaw with the thumb and forefinger of one hand—the thumb in the fish's mouth and forefinger crooked under its chin—and work the lure loose with the other. You can do this with the fish in or out of the water, either dangling vertically from your hand in the open air or lying just under the surface of the water beside your boat as you work. Of course, doing it with the fish still in the water will be easier on the fish, even if harder on your aching back. It's sometimes simpler to get the hook out if you use needle-nose fishing pliers to give you better leverage.

The correct way to hold a bass is by grasping its lower jaw. This temporarily paralyzes it while you remove the hook.

With non-bass species, the best way to hold a fish while working the hook loose is to grasp it with one hand saddle-style over the back behind the head, with your thumb over one gill cover and four fingers over the other. Pressure on the gill covers seems to have the same mildly paralyzing effect as lipping does on a bass, and keeps the fish from flapping around so much while you fiddle with the lure. *Never* try to immobilize a fish you plan to release by pressing your fingers over its eyes, or inserting your fingers inside its gills. This is likely to injure the fish badly enough that releasing it would be an exercise in futility. Grab a fish that way only if you intend to eat it or mount it.

After removing the hook, most of the time you only have to let go and watch your prize swim free

Needle-nosed pliers are useful for removing hooks from a bass's bony jaw.

Left   Wayne Izumi holds a smallmouth by its lower jaw.

Right   He gently puts it back into the water.

to fight again another day. Once in a while, though, a particularly determined battler may have so exhausted itself that it will need a little help recovering its strength and equilibrium before release. In this case, after removing the hook, gently hold the fish with one hand at the tail and the other under the stomach and move it slowly forward (never backward) in the water. The water passing through its gills as you move it will provide revivifying oxygen and after one or two passes your prize will give a lash of its tail and blast off at full throttle. This treatment may also be needed if a fish has been kept in a livewell for some time, even if the well is aerated.

If a fish has been fatally exhausted during the fight to land it, or has swallowed the hook and sustained injury to its internal organs, releasing it would be useless. In this case, it's better to keep it and fry it up for dinner, than to let it go only to float away, belly-up in the water. It should also go without saying that gaff hooks, salmon tailers and other such paraphernalia don't mesh very well with catch-and-release fishing, for whatever species. The idea is to release a healthy fish, not a maimed cripple.

NINE

BASS **TOURNAMENTS**

Competitive tournament fishing is a way of life for me—a physical and intellectual challenge, a fascinating source of knowledge and a natural high all wrapped up together. I'm as addicted to it as a Formula One racer to speed or a rock climber to heights and tricky hand-holds.

But I guess it comes naturally. The first bass tournament I ever entered was the very first one in Canada, and it was organized by my Dad, Joe Izumi. Dad worked as a chef at the hospital in Chatham, Ontario, and back in the early '70s one of his friends there, Murray King, had one of the old, tri-hull bass boats and used to fish in tournaments along the northern U.S. bass circuit. Tournaments were just coming into their own in the States then, and he talked them up to my Dad.

Well, when Dad got enthusiastic about something it had a way of happening, and before long he'd transplanted the concept to Canada, to Rondeau Bay on Lake Erie. I fished that first tournament in a 14-foot, shallow-draft aluminum boat with a six-horse motor and with a local angler, Bob English, as my partner. We didn't finish in the money, but I've been in tournaments ever since and have seen their whole history in Canada.

It's hard to describe what tournament life is like. If you've never tried it, the things you hear about it may seem bizarre, like a description of the customs in some exotic country. And if you're

Wayne and Bob holding their trophies — another tournament win.

already part of it, it's so much a second nature kind of thing that you hardly ever think about what makes it special.

My involvement in a tournament typically begins weeks in advance, as I check out the charts and maps, listen to the gossip and opinions circulating among the other pros and talk over plans with my brother Wayne. A few days before the tournament, I drive down to the site in my van, towing the 18-foot Ranger, and try to get in some on-the-water practice. The other guys are already beginning to arrive, checking into their motels, and the conversation in local restaurants is dominated by fishing, fishing and more fishing. People are swapping stories, checking out one another's boats and rigs and psyching out the competition as they move out on the water, looking for the good spots. If the fishing is good and the bass are hitting, we're all praying for the weather to hold and the cold fronts to stay away. It's relatively relaxed, practice fishing—the formal competition hasn't actually begun—but your antennae are out when you're on the water.

The night before blast-off, I'm typically charged up like a battery, crackling with anticipation. In the early days, I'd get so nervous I'd actually be sick, but now I just hum like a high-voltage wire. It's important, if you can, to get a good night's sleep, but I usually don't get to bed until 10:30 or 11 P.M. because there's so much to do. Wayne and I are up sharpening hooks, getting extra lures out, spooling line, looking over the maps, getting food and soft drinks packed for the next day's lunch. If it's still light, we'll be checking gear in the boat.

When you wake up, it's 4 A.M. and that's *early*, but everyone's dressed and wolfing down their eggs, and pretty soon they're all down at the docks or marina, putting their tackle on board and warming up their motors. I like to listen to loud, upbeat music around then; it sort of gears me up.

Then comes blast-off. In Canada, many tournaments still use a shotgun start, with 50 to 100 boats lined up revving, and then taking off in flights with a big roar and spray, slapping over the waves at 60 mph to get to their prime spots. It can be dangerous with all those buck-and-a-halfs around you, but you're so excited it doesn't matter, roaring off to your own spot, wondering if the fish will still be where they were yesterday.

The actual day on the water can be tough. It's not like pleasure fishing, where you only go out when the weather's fine and the fish are biting. In tournaments, you're out there in all kinds of weather—pouring rain, thunderstorms, hail, wind, cold fronts that turn your lips blue, blistering hot days—no matter what, you fish. I've been out in storms where the air is so charged that if you're using a graphite rod, holding it parallel to the water, and then lift the tip up, you can hear "Zzzzzzz," crackling, and the hair rises on the back of your neck. When you cast, your line floats in the air, with a bow to it, because of the static electricity. There'll be a big clap of thunder, and maybe, right in the middle of all that, you'll get a bass on. It's wild!

Other times, it will be eight or nine hours on the water with the sun belting down, draining your energy. In one New York tournament, we had to run 120 miles in a morning to the tournament site, fish a few hours and then turn around for the 120-mile trip back. We were six hours in transit.

Every tournament is different, too. I've been as impressed by some with 20 boats entered as some with 200 boats. You never know what will happen, what your partner will be like or what conditions you'll run into. You're learning constantly, from your partner, from the fish, from everything that happens—and some weird things happen.

Once, I caught a largemouth that weighed-in at 5.8 pounds, and released it near the weigh-in spot.

The next day one of my competitors was fishing the riprap up near the scales and caught the same fish—5.8 pounds. I've seen times when, in the last 15 minutes of a tournament, guys who were really getting worried about being skunked suddenly caught their limit of fish. In the last five minutes you can catch your biggest fish of the day, or you can experience the opposite extreme. Once, on Balsam Lake, Ontario, Wayne and I came on a large group of four-and five-pounders, but no matter what we tried they just wouldn't hit. We could see them with our Polaroid glasses, following our crankbaits right up to the boat. But they wouldn't take anything. It was mind-boggling. We ended up weighing in something like two pounds that day. Another time, on the Bay of Quinte, they wouldn't stop hitting. It was a stupendous day. We weighed in 45 pounds with 12 largemouth and won the tournament.

A lot depends on getting along with your fishing partner, and that's something I've learned over the years from experience. In the United States, most pro tournaments are draw-for-partner and you never know who you'll get. It's a great learning situation because you have the opportunity to fish with all sorts of people and watch different techniques in action. Your boat partner is actually competing against you as an individual in the tournament, and yet you have to cooperate if you want to get anything done. In Canada, most people prefer to choose their partner, rather than fish with a stranger, and here I usually fish with Wayne. That way I have it both ways, fishing sometimes with a person I know well and get along with, and sometimes with an unknown who might be right off the wall.

I have to say, though, that most of the people on the pro bass tournament circuit are good, down-to-earth fishermen and are willing to work with you. Courtesy is the rule. It's expected. Once in a while you'll get a cheater or a guy who tries to edge you

A fair-sized smallmouth will soon be swimming in the lake after it has been weighed in.

out. At one walleye tournament in Ontario, a guy tried to bring in live bait. He had sandwiches wrapped up and between the slices of bread there were nightcrawlers! But he got kicked out. Another guy might try to crowd you by keeping his boat's bow pointed to a good spot and standing up front in your way, so you have to stretch from the back of the boat. But these guys don't last long. A pro would just cast right by them, "give 'em line burns on their ears," we say, and there are a thousand tricks of the trade an experienced man can use to even the odds. In the end, it's better to work with your partner, than against him, and to maintain a positive attitude.

I remember one of the earliest tournaments I fished in, where I didn't do either. I was fishing at Rice Lake, Ontario, with a good friend of mine from Blenheim, Joe Stewart, and the first day of the tournament we did really well. We used buzzbaits and must have caught a good 25 or 30 bass. We kept the biggest and at weigh-in we had 16 pounds for six

Lined up after a long day of tournament fishing to weigh in the catch.

fish and were leading the tournament. But we didn't use our heads. We forgot, first, that in a tournament the name of the game is versatility, and second, that you can't allow yourself to develop a bad attitude.

On the second day, we went to the same spots we'd fished on day one and used the same method—buzzbaits. We figured it worked once, it'll work again. But we'd burnt those spots out, and the fish weren't hitting on buzzbaits anymore. At first we were too stubborn to change and kept on buzzing. We wasted a good two hours that way and caught one fish. But finally we switched to a jig and pig and plastic worms. We started getting hits again, but now our attitude was poor. Psychologically, we didn't have our act together and the confidence just wasn't there. Strange things started happening.

We would get really big fish on, but lose them, in a whole series of incredible flukes—four-and-a-half-pounders, three-pounders, we lost more fish than I'd ever seen. I caught a three-and-a-half-pound fish under a log, but didn't set the hook right and it spit the lure. Joe caught a four-pounder on a plastic worm, a largemouth, but it went under the boat and then came up and jumped three feet into the air and spit the worm. We were both being careless, not concentrating, and when we started losing those fish we got wrangling, too. It ended up we almost had a fist fight out in the boat, even though we're the best of friends.

We finished that day with two fish, and took ninth place. Meanwhile, my brother, who'd weighed in a respectable 15 pounds the first day and just kept on fishing methodically the second, came in with another 15 pounds and took first place. It was all in the attitude.

My attitude now is that I enjoy competing and it's the competitiveness that draws me to tournaments. But basically I'm in there for three reasons: 1) to have fun; 2) to learn and; 3) to win—in that order. The learning part is important to all my other work, and teaches me things I can pass on in my television show, in articles and seminars. If I didn't fish tournaments I wouldn't know a quarter of what I do now about the sport.

But the fun part is undeniably a tremendous incentive, too. It's a thrill for me when weigh-in time comes at the end of a day, and you see what everybody else has been doing. When you pull up to the dock and take your place in line you're full of anticipation, eager to see what's going on. You're thinking: "How'd so-and-so do? Wow, look at that bag of big fish!" And if you have a good catch yourself, there's that feeling of personal accomplishment. On the first day, you're noticing things like the color of the fish caught, and thinking: "That guy's got a bunch of dark ones, so he must have got 'em out of heavy cover. I'll have to try the thick stuff tomorrow." Or: "This fella's leading with six fish, but five of them are one-and-a-half-pounders and only one's over five pounds. That means he's probably not on big fish and you can still overtake him tomorrow." On the final day, the weigh-in decides everything and you're waiting to see if you've won.

Somebody once asked me what it feels like to win a tournament, and I answered in one word: Great.

So yes, it's a great way to make a living, but that's not all tournament fishing is. A lot of conservative fishermen don't like tournaments. They say it takes the fun out of fishing by making it too competitive and doesn't do anything for the sport. Well, they're wrong. I think what I've already described is proof enough that tournaments are fun with a capital "F," and the catch-and-release philosophy they promote is good for the sport everywhere, promoting good conservation practice.

But equally important is the role of tournaments in improving our knowledge of fish and in serving as a laboratory for the research and development of new techniques and equipment. An astronaut once justified the expense of flying to the moon partly on the basis of the spin-off technologies such a project developed, in medicine, engineering and so forth. It's the same with pro tournaments. They're laboratories where the most skilled anglers in North America gather together under the harshest and most varied conditions possible to field-test the very latest equipment. What they learn is of value to every man or woman who wets a line. The modern bass boat evolved almost entirely from modifications made under tournament conditions. Nearly all of the most recent innovations in tackle—particularly in bait-casting tackle—came as a result of things anglers discovered in competition. The art of pattern fishing, hundreds of nuances in the use and meaning of structure, close observations of fish behavior in adverse weather conditions—the list of things tournament participants have discovered is endless. And the top tournament pros are sharing their knowledge with other fishermen, in seminars, books, tapes, on television and in person.

No, I won't let anybody tell me tournaments are anything but a positive benefit to the ancient art of angling.

And besides, I like them. Somebody once asked me what I'd do if I won a million-dollar lottery and didn't have to work for a living anymore. Well, I know a millionaire, a Texas oil man who made so much money he doesn't have to do anything. We met as draw partners in a bass boat, and he said he fishes a bass tournament every week. I think he has the right idea. If I were him, I'd spend my time that way, too. I wouldn't do anything else.

Well, almost anything else.

The largest bass of the tournament.

GLOSSARY

bait-casting outfit—a level-wind, revolving spool reel usually mounted on a pistol grip rod

breakline—a change in depth or vegetation in a body of water

bucktail—a jig dressed with deer hair

buzzbait (buzzer)—a topwater lure with a buzzing sound and fast action that irritates fish into striking

catch-and-release fishing—catching a fish and then returning it unharmed to the water

cofilament line—a nylon line with a polyester core

color-selector—a device that measures water clarity and light refraction and then indicates which lure color to use

crankbait—a lipped lure, usually resembling a bait fish, that can be worked at various depths

drag control—an adjustable clutch used as a braking system to control the turning action of the reel

electric thruster—a small foot-pedal- or hand-controlled motor

fingerling—fish up to one year of age

flasher unit—a depth-finder using a dial and flashing lights to indicate depth, bottom structure and the location of fish

flipping—an underhanded pendulum-type cast used for catching fish in heavy cover

fry—newly hatched fish

graph—a depth-finder using a roll of lined graph paper and a needle to trace the contour of the bottom and to indicate the location of fish

graphite—a form of carbon used to make rods

grip—the handle of a rod

hook-set—setting the hook in the fish's jaw after it has struck the bait

jig—a single hook, lead-headed lure made in many different weights, colors and shapes

jig and pig (jig and pork)—a jig with a piece of pork rind attached to it

kill switch—a device that automatically shuts off a boat's engine if the operator falls overboard

lateral line—a dark band running from the head to the tail along each side of a largemouth bass *leader*—a wire strand used to prevent fish with sharp teeth from severing the line

limit—the legal number and size of fish that can be caught in a designated period of time

lipping—grasping a fish by its lower jaw

mag reel—a reel that uses magnets to control spool speed while casting

monofilament line—a nylon line

mudline—an area where the muddy water from a river or canal meets the clear water of a lake

pheromones—hormone-like chemicals that transmit messages from one member of a species to another

plug—a wood or plastic lure made in many different weights, colors and shapes

popper—a topwater lure that pops on the surface of the water as it is retrieved

presentation—a specific technique used to catch fish; for example, flipping and cranking

riprap—a man-made wall or foundation of stones or pieces of concrete in water

roving—graphite fiber strands of uneven lengths twisted into loose braids; used to make rods

side-cast—a cast made horizontal to the surface of the water

solunar tables—tables that list major and minor activity or feeding periods for fish and wildlife at various latitudes and at various times of the year, based on the movements of the sun and moon

spinnerbait (spinner)—a safety-pin-design lure with a revolving blade and a lead-headed hook beneath it

spinning outfit—an underslung stationary spool reel mounted on a rod

spoon—a lure made of metal and shaped like a spoon

structure fishing—fishing by identifying the movements of fish from one type of underwater terrain to another

tackle—fishing gear—rod, reel, line and lures and anything related to them

terminal tackle—tackle affixed to the end of a line; for example, snaps, swivels and leaders

uni-directional tape—flat strips of many parallel graphite fibers held together with epoxy

weedless plug—a lure with the hook point covered to allow it to move through the cover without becoming entangled

INDEX